Money, Misery, Madness

The Book of Financial Disaster Quotations

Money, Misery, Madness

The Book of Financial Disaster Quotations

Compiled by
Eugene Weber

B. T. BATSFORD LIMITED · LONDON

© Eugene Weber 1997
First published 1997

Published by B T Batsford Ltd,
583 Fulham Road,
London SW6 5BY

Printed by
Redwood Books
Trowbridge
Wiltshire

ISBN 0 7134 8350 4

A CIP catalogue record for this book
is available from The British Library

MONEY, MISERY, MADNESS

INTRODUCTION AND ACKNOWLEDGEMENTS

This collection has been compiled to coincide with the anniversary of the 1987 world-wide share price crash. It is a timely reminder, when the Wall Street and London stock markets are at all time highs, that the good days don't last forever.

Although many of the quotations are about various market crashes, the book includes comments on different kinds of economic, personal and financial disasters from inflation to Lloyd's of London and ruin brought about by criminal activity.

Politicians have spoken of the dangers of inflation and how, if left unchecked, it can lead to the disintegration of society. It's only when you read about the consequences of the great German inflation of the 1920s and its effect on society that you realise how bad it can get. The Nazi party might not have arisen had it not been for inflation.

For all those lovers of *schadenfreude*, the enjoyment of other's misfortune, the Lloyd's of London quotations will be hard to beat. Nobody cares about the ruined Names and they are perceived by the public at large as a people who got what they deserved.

When all is said and done, it is hard to understand how we continue to make the same financial mistakes again and again. People still think that markets will rise and rise and ordinary people are still persuaded to invest their hard-earned money in dubious enterprises proposed by even more dubious characters.

A more ominous sign today is that even the most respectable of companies are prepared to use tricks as old as the hills to sell dodgy pensions to unsuspecting customers. These companies have been accused of "mis-selling" (how about that for a euphemism) but surely fraud is the more appropriate word.

For whatever reason you read this book I hope you find something here which will enlighten, inform, or amuse.

I would like to express my gratitude to the following people who helped me to compile this collection. Matin Liu for inspiration. Paul Hannon, Sarah Kelly and Theo Weber for research and Gunni Muschenheim of the German Institute in London. I am especially indebted to Sr. Eilish Weber for her invaluable research in the United States.

Eugene Weber
London
September 1997

1

WARNING SIGNS

Boom times create abnormalities when billions of pounds fly through the air with the greatest of ease.

> *Larry Adler, founder, Fire & All Risks Insurance*

Of all the mysteries of the stock exchange there is none so impenetrable as why there should be a buyer for everyone who seeks to sell.

> *Prof. John Kenneth Galbraith*

I'm sure a crash like 1929 will happen again. The only thing is that one doesn't know when. All it takes for another collapse is for the memories of the last insanity to dull.

> *Prof. John Kenneth Galbraith*

There is nothing like the ticker tape except a woman. Nothing that promises hour after hour, day after day such golden developments, nothing that disappoints so often or occasionally fulfils with such unbelievable passionate magnificence.

> *Walter Knowleton Gutman, investment adviser*

You must never confuse genius with a bull market.

> *Nick Leslau, chief executive of Burford*

A company for carrying on an undertaking of great advantage, but nobody to know what it is.

> *Part of the prospectus for a company at the time of the South Sea Bubble*

I like to think that if I woke up tomorrow and it was October 1929, I would still be comfortable.

> *Robert Holmes à Court, the Australian-based financier,*
> *one month before the 1987 crash in which he was a major*
> *loser.*

O hush thee, my babe, granny's bought some more shares,
Daddy's gone to play with the bulls and the bears,
Mother's buying on tips and she simply can't lose,
And baby shall have some expensive new shoes.

> *A popular ditty summing up the mood of euphoria prior to the*
> *1929 crash.*

I can feel it coming, S.E.C. or not, a whole new round of disastrous speculation, with all the familiar stages in order – blue-chip boom, then a fad for secondary issues, then an over-the-counter play, then another garbage market in new issues, and finally the inevitable crash. I don't know when it will come, but I can feel it coming, and damn it, I don't know what to do about it.

> *Bernard J Lasker, then chairman of the New York Stock*
> *Exchange in 1970.*

By the summer of 1929 the market not only dominated the news, it also dominated the culture. That recherche minority which at other times has acknowledged its interest in St. Thomas Aquinas, Proust, psychoanalysis and psychosomatic medicine then spoke of United Corporation, United Founders, and Steel. Only the most aggressive of the eccentrics maintained their detachment from the market and their interest in autosuggestion or communism.

> *Prof. John Kenneth Galbraith*

Statesmen forgot their Politics, Lawyers the Bar, Merchants their Traffic, Physicians their Patients, Tradesmen their Shops, Debtors of Quality their Creditors, Divines the Pulpit and even Women themselves their Pride and Vanity.

Viscount Erleigh on the South Sea Bubble

Financial capacity and political perspicacity are inversely correlated. Long-run salvation by men of business has never been highly regarded if it means disturbance of orderly life and convenience in the present. So inaction will be advocated in the present even though it means deep trouble in the future. Here, at least equally with communism, lie the threat to capitalism. It is what causes men who know that things are going quite wrong to say that things are fundamentally sound.

Prof. John Kenneth Galbraith

Occasional outbreaks of those two super-contagious diseases, fear and greed, will forever occur in the investment community. The timing of these epidemics... the market aberrations produced... will be equally unpredictable, both as to duration and degree. Therefore we never try to anticipate the arrival or departure of either... we simply attempt to be fearful when others are greedy and to be greedy only when others are fearful.

Warren Buffett

This market is not discounting the future but the hereafter.

Max Winkler, economist, in 1928

A mania is a mania, and the experts are caught in it just as the public is.

Marc Faber, investment guru

There has been a long history of the proffering of exotic devices for the fleecing of the public. Today's fashionable vehicle is the ostrich farming scam.

Mr. Justice Lightman granting a petition for the winding up of the Ostrich Farming Corporation.

The object of the author in the following pages has been to collect the most remarkable instances of those moral epidemics which have been excited, sometimes by one cause and sometimes by another, and to show how easily the masses have been led astray, and how imitative and gregarious men are, even in their infatuations and crimes.

Part of the preface to the book Extraordinary Popular Delusions and the Madness of Crowds, by Charles Mackay, which was published in 1841.

Money, again, has often been a cause of the delusion of the multitudes. Sober nations have all at once become desperate gamblers, and risked almost their existence upon the turn of a piece of paper.

Charles Mackay

The public enthusiasm, which had been so long rising, could not resist a vision so splendid. At least three hundred thousand applications were made for the fifty thousand new shares, and Law's house in the Rue de Quincampoix was beset from morning to night by the eager applicants. As it was impossible to satisfy them all, it was several weeks before a list of the fortunate new stockholders could be made out, during which time the public impatience rose to a pitch of frenzy. Dukes, marquises, counts, with their duchesses, marchionesses, and countesses, waited in the streets for hours every day before Mr

Law's door to know the result. At last, to avoid the jostling of the plebeian crowd, which, to the number of thousands, filled the whole thoroughfare, they took apartments in the adjoining houses, that they might be continually near the temple whence the new Plutus was diffusing wealth. Every day the value of the old shares increased, and the fresh applications, induced by the golden dreams of the whole nation, became so numerous that it was deemed advisable to create no less than three hundred thousand new shares, at five thousand livres each, in order that the regent might take advantage of the popular enthusiasm to pay off the national debt. For this purpose, the sum of fifteen hundred millions of livres was necessary. Such was the eagerness of the nation, that thrice the sum would have been subscribed if the government had authorised it.

> *Charles Mackay, writing in the 1840s on John Law's Mississippi Scheme.*

The highest and the lowest classes were alike filled with a vision of boundless wealth. There was not a person of note among the aristocracy, with the exception of the Duke of St. Simon and Marshal Vikkars, who was not engaged in buying or selling stock. People of every age and sex and condition in life speculated in the rise and fall of the Mississippi bonds. The Rue de Quincampoix was the grand resort of the jobbers, and it being a narrow, inconvenient street, accidents continually occurred in it, from the tremendous pressure of the crowd. Houses in it, worth, in ordinary times, a thousand livres of yearly rent, yielded as much as twelve or sixteen thousand. A cobbler, who had a stall in it, gained about two hundred livres a day by letting it out, and furnishing writing materials to brokers and their clients. The story goes that a hunchbacked man who stood in the street gained considerable sums by lending his hump as a writing desk to the eager speculators. The great concourse of persons who assembled to do business brought a still greater concourse of spectators. These again drew all the thieves and immoral characters of Paris to the spot, and constant riots and disturbances took place.

Charles Mackay

At length corruption, like a general flood,
So long by watchful ministers withstood
Shall deluge all; and avarice creeping on,
Spread, like a low-born mist, and blot the sun.
Statesman and patriot ply alike the stocks,
Peeress and butler share alike the box;
The judge shall job, the bishop bite the town,
And mighty dukes pack cards for half-a-crown.
See Britain sunk in lucre's sordid charms…

Alexander Pope on the South Sea Bubble

"All this is madness," cries a sober sage:
But who, my friend, has reason in his rage ?
"The ruling passion, be it what it will,
The ruling passion conquers reason still."

Alexander Pope on the South Sea Bubble

When the rest of the world are mad, we must imitate them in some measure.

John Biddulph Martin, banker, on the South Sea Bubble

A cancer has been spreading in our industry. Too much money is coming together with too many young people who have little or no institutional memory or sense of tradition and who are under enormous economic pressure to perform in the glare of Hollywood-like publicity. The combination makes for speculative excess at best, illegality at worst.

New York banker Felix Rohatyn on the 1980s

The bigger the headquarters the more decadent the company
Sir James Goldsmith

The sucker has always tried to get something for nothing, and the appeal in all booms is always frankly to the gambling instinct aroused by cupidity and spurred by a pervasive prosperity. People who look for easy money invariably pay for the privilege of proving conclusively that it cannot be found on this sordid earth.
Edwin Lefèvre, business writer

It is just when you are most successful that you are most vulnerable. That is when you make your biggest mistakes.
Roger Foster, founder of Apricot Computers

Rolls Royces with personalised number plates, a fountain in the reception area; a flag pole; the Queen's Award for Industry (UK companies only); a chairman who is honoured for his services to industry – every industry but his own; a salesman or engineer as chief executive; a recent move into modern offices.
Bill Mackey, former managing partner of Ernst &Whinney

All these ego-feeding activities – the long hours in the limousine, the sky-larking in the corporate jet, the collection of press clippings, the unnecessary speeches – feed the corporate sickness and one way or another make a corporate problem out of what had been an otherwise perfectly competent, even brilliant executive.
Harold Geneen, then boss of ITT

The more luxurious the luncheon rooms at headquarters, the more inefficient the business.
Roland Franklin, founder, Pembridge Investments

Sell the shares when the chairman or chief executive becomes president of the CBI.

Sir Mark Weinberg, company director

If a stock doesn't act right don't touch it; because, being unable to tell precisely what is wrong, you cannot tell which way it is going. No diagnosis, no prognosis. No prognosis, no profit.

Edwin Lefèvre, business writer

The speculator's chief enemies are always boring from within. It is inseparable from human nature to hope and to fear. In speculation when the market goes against you, you hope that every day will be the last day – and you lose more than you should had you not listened to hope – to the same allay that is so potent a success-bringer to empire builders and pioneers, big and little. And when the market goes your way you become fearful that the next day will take away your profit, and you get out too soon. Fear keeps you from making as much money as you ought to. The successful trader has to fight these two deep-seated instincts. He has to reverse what you might call his natural impulses. Instead of hoping he must fear; instead of fearing he must hope.

Edwin Lefèvre

Nobles, citizens, farmers, mechanics, seamen, footmen, maid servants, even chimney sweeps and old clothes women dabbled in tulips.

Charles Mackay on the Dutch tulip mania in the 17th century

The overbearing insolence of ignorant men, who had risen to sudden wealth by successful gambling, made men of true gentility of mind and manners blush that gold should have the power to raise the unworthy in the scale of society. The haughtiness of some of these 'cyphering cits' as they were termed by Sir Richard Steele, was remembered against them in their days of adversity.

Charles Mckay

All nations with a capitalist mode of production are seized periodically by a feverish attempt to make money without the mediation of the process of production.

Karl Marx

Subscribers here by thousands float
And jostle one another down,
Each paddling in his leaky boat,
And here they fish for gold and drown...

Meantime, secure on Garraway cliffs,
A savage race, by shipwrecks fed,
Lie waiting for the foundered skiffs,
And strip the bodies of the dead.

Jonathan Swift on the South Sea Bubble

When a company hires an expensive consultant to give it a new logo and a more corporate image, wise investors often take the opportunity to sell. More often than not, new images are like new headquarters buildings: evidence of the fact that the company's top management have lost sight of their real job.

Tim Jackson, business writer

Most management people I know still believe that the Bible begins with the words: "In the beginning God created stable exchange rates."

Peter Drucker, management guru

Long periods of prosperity usually end in scandal.

Prof. George Taucher

All distinctions of party, religion, sex, character and circumstances were swallowed up in this universal concern or on some such pecuniary project. Exchange Alley was filled with a strange concourse of statesmen and clergymen, churchmen and dissenters, Whigs and Tories, physicians, lawyers, tradesmen and even multitudes of females. All other professions and employments were utterly neglected; and the people's attention wholly engrossed by this and other chimerical schemes which were known by the denomination of bubbles.

Tobias Smollett on the South Sea Bubble

Every age in the stock market reinvents the wheel, convinced it has created something new and quite wonderful while completely ignoring what happened to the old wheel.

Mihir Bose, business writer

Gambling in stock has become a national disease. This malady reaches all classes of people, from preachers to stable boys. Only a short time ago in all circles everyone was talking about prohibition. Whenever people met the prohibition question in its varied angles was the subject of discussion. Now when people meet, whether it be business men or labouring men, whether ladies in their social gatherings or sewing circles, or shop girls, the stock market with its wild vagaries is the topic anxiously and too often tragically canvassed. I have had many letters from various parts of the United States. from poor deluded people who have lost their limited savings in the destructive gambling maelstrom.

Senator William King during the crash of 1929

Nowhere does history indulge in repetitions so often or so uniformly as in Wall Street. When you read contemporary accounts of booms or panics the one thing that strikes you most forcibly is how little either stock speculation or stock speculators today differ from yesterday. The game does not change and neither does human nature.

Edwin Lefèvre

History demonstrates that participants in financial markets are susceptible to waves of optimism. Excessive optimism sows the seeds of its own reversal in the form of imbalances that tend to grow over time.

Alan Greenspan, Federal Reserve chairman

The pursuit of fashion to the point of mania had indeed been the hallmark of financial institutions – and especially banks – throughout the ages.

Sir Kit McMahon, former chairman of the Midland Bank

Men, it has been well said, think in herds; it will be seen that they go mad in herds, while they only recover their senses slowly and one by one.

Charles Mackay

Some in clandestine companies combine;
Erect new stocks to trade beyond the line;
With air and empty names beguile the town,
And raise new credits first, then cry 'em down;
Divide the empty nothing into shares,
And set the crowd together by the ears.

Daniel Defoe, on the South Sea Bubble

There is something about inside information which seems to paralyse a man's reasoning powers.

Bernard Baruch, US financier

People forget that today's junk is often tomorrow's blue chip

Michael Milken, creator of junk bonds

When you see business execs. helicoptering to the golf course, waiters discussing the merits of Intel versus Applied Materials, 22-year-olds in suspenders smoking cigars and drinking. Martinis, and houses in the suburbs selling way over the asking price – then you know that the referee has brought the whistle to his lips and is about to blow. The game is nearly over.

James K Glassman, journalist

2

BANKS

Keep your peckers up.

> *Peter Baring, chairman of Barings Bank, to staff during the crisis*

He had a lot of balls but no bearings.

> *A broker on Nick Leeson*

I hope they hang him.

> *A City worker on Nick Leeson*

A great nemesis has overtaken Croesus.

> *Tom Baring during the bank's crisis in 1890*

Lord Revelstoke (Barings' chairman) had rashly and credulously put all he had into these Argentine mines or works, and had been cheated by the Argentine agents who had come to him.

> *Queen Victoria on the Barings crisis in 1890*

If Mr Leeson goes to prison while the former board of Barings continue going to Glyndebourne the bitterest of tastes will be left behind.

> *Daily Telegraph editorial*

I knew I had lost millions of pounds, but I didn't know how much. I was too frightened to find out – the numbers scared me to death,

> *Nick Leeson*

I don't think of myself as a criminal. I was trying to correct a situation. And however naive and stupid this might sound, I was always working in the best interests of the bank.

Nick Leeson

The Mad Hatter's Tea Party.

Peter Norris, former chief executive officer at Barings Bank, describing the atmosphere at the bank in the days leading up to the crash.

I am very sorry gentlemen, our investor is not willing to proceed.

Eddie George, governor of the Bank of England, announcing to the group of bankers gathered to try and save Barings that he had failed to rescue the bank.

What's the difference between Elvis and Nick Leeson? Nick Leeson's definitely dead.

A joke doing the rounds during the Barings collapse.

I was so shocked when I first saw the headline in the Borneo Times that I couldn't bring myself to pick up the paper. When I heard the bank was closing I just thought "Oh, my God." My legs started shaking, it was like going into an exam. I knew Barings had lost a lot of money, but I never imagined they were on the brink of disaster.

Nick Leeson

My sincere apologies for the predicament that I have left you in. It was neither my intention nor aim for this to happen but the pressures, both business and personal, have become too much to bear and after receiving medical advice, have affected my health to the extent that a breakdown is imminent.

Nick Leeson

There is perhaps no record of a bank fraud existent of which the perpetrator was not honest yesterday.

James S. Gibbons, writer

Because we're independent, people come to us when they're in trouble. They come to auntie and auntie helps them. They find us wise, sympathetic and helpful – but not rich.

Sir George Blunden, then deputy governor of the Bank of England

I regard the 1973/74 collapse as a disaster for all men of enterprise and a victory for the people who do nothing and want to do nothing. The grouse moor brigade is being baled out by the Bank of England.

Oliver Jessel, the founder of Jessel Securities, on the secondary banking crisis which at one point threatened the whole banking system.

I am far from alone in my youth and inexperience. The world of international banking is now full of aggressive, bright, but hopelessly inexperienced lenders in their mid-twenties. They travel the world like itinerant brushmen, filling loan quotas, peddling financial wares and living high on the hog. Their bosses are often bright but hopelessly inexperienced twenty-nine year old vice-presidents with wardrobes from Brooks Brothers, MBAs from Wharton or Stanford and so little credit training that they would have trouble with a simple retail instalment loan.

S C Gwynne, banker

We foreign bankers are for the free market system when we are out to make a buck and believe in the state when we're about to lose a buck.

Banker quoted in the Wall Street Journal.

I think one of my biggest failings is that I allow people to get away with too much. And, you know, I'm always trying to please.

Nick Leeson

I don't regard myself as a criminal. I also almost see myself as a victim of what I am, in that I have tried to help people too much.

Nick Leeson

The biggest crime I am guilty of is trying to protect people and ensure that the bonuses they expected were paid and it is this that led to the escalation of the problem and the offences of which I now stand accused.

Nick Leeson

For the first time since my arrest, I realised that I was glad to have played my part in the fiasco rather than theirs. I was happier in my prison cell than they were, sitting at home nursing their credibility back to pieces and always knowing what their friends were saying behind their backs. Fuck 'em I thought. I could face my family and friends and look them in the eye. I had nothing to hide.

Nick Leeson

It was advantageous to me that the senior people in London who were arranging these payments didn't understand the basic administration of futures and options and that was the biggest failing.

Nick Leeson

It is difficult to get a fix on the motivation of this fellow.

Peter Baring on Nick Leeson

A bank lives on credit. Till it is trusted it is nothing; and when it ceases to be trusted it turns to nothing.
>   *Walter Bagehot*

The City is becoming enveloped deeper and deeper in a baleful, mysterious crisis. Day by day thick clouds gather over the Stock Markets. ....This slow-killing agony has been going on now for about two months without coming to a head. The worst kind of fever would reach its climax in less time.
>   *The Financial Times on the Baring crisis in 1890*

If you see a Genevan banker jump out of the window, follow him for there is sure to be money where he lands.
>   *Voltaire*

If I owe a million dollars, then I am lost. But if I owe fifty billion, the bankers are lost.
>   *Celso Ming, Brazilian economist*

They don't know the difference between international finance and buying goods from the Cho Hom market.
>   *An Asian banker on Vietnam's struggling national bank*

He seemed very good at what he did.
>   *Daiwa Bank president Akira Fujita on Toshihide Iguchi, the trader accused of running up losses of $1.1 billion trading US bonds.*

The Bank of Crooks and Criminals.
>   *BCCI*

Shout if left out.

> *Peter Baring to staff who felt uninformed by management during the Barings crisis.*

Every day you are walking across a tight-rope across Niagara. You have no control over the wind and at any moment it can change. When it does, you're fucked.

> *A trader at Barings after the collapse*

He is creating an image of himself as the Rogue Trader – when, in reality, he is just an accountant who cooked the books. And a crap trader.

> *Ron Baker, Nick Leeson's former boss*

Mr George is chuckling. Maybe if you lost a slice of your salary every time you lost a bank, Mr George, maybe you wouldn't be chuckling.

> *Diane Abbott MP to Bank of England governor Eddie George at a Treasury select committee session on the collapse of Barings Bank.*

Whatever you think of him, he put Pakistani banking on the map of the world.

> *A Karachi banker following the death of Agha Hasan Abedi, the founder of BCCI*

Even Colombian drug barons don't throw that sort of money around without a few signatures.

> *A merchant banker on the Barings fiasco*

Fingering Leeson alone is like blaming a lance-corporal for the outcome of the First World War.

> *A banker on the Barings fiasco*

Heron is a horse with a broken leg. When we saw the cost of fixing the leg, the option of shooting the horse suddenly became much more attractive.

A banker on the troubled Heron Corporation

It's the most difficult job I know as a central banker to be able to make up your mind whether you can allow this institution to collapse without worrying about system failure.

Brian Quinn, then head of supervision at the Bank of England, on the Barings Bank disaster

There were days when I could lose £25-30 million. There were days when I made £50 million... Not every day is a down day.

Nick Leeson

He ran away, true to a dealer's instinct.

An American bank official on Nick Leeson

I can guarantee to you that I can count. I don't think that was one of the reasons for the collapse of Barings.

Nick Leeson

Sometimes I could not hold the bags because they were so heavy. It was like pulling a sack of garbage.

Former BCCI bagman Aziz Raymond

If we close a bank every time we find an example or two of fraud we would have rather fewer banks.

Robin Leigh-Pemberton, then governor of the Bank of England, on the BCCI scandal

I don't hold myself responsible because I have not had anything to do with the affairs of BCCI for the past three years.
Agha Hasan Abedi, founder of BCCI

The Bank of Crooks and Cocaine International.
BCCI

It's terrible – all my money. I'm going to go for a drink now.
A BCCI customer

When I joined the international group we had two branches: the London branch, which was losing money, and the Paris branch, which was losing money, but elegantly.
Walter Wriston, banker

My shelf life is remarkable. I never walk the streets of New York without seeing somebody I knew or who knew me. The moral of that story is always be with your own wife.
Walter Wriston in his retirement

Americans are still reasonably parochial. They'd rather make a bad loan in Texas than a good loan in Brazil.
Walter Wriston

The difference between a skinflint banker and a reckless lender is a recession.
Walter Wriston

Have you ever watched a rugby football match when one of the players loses his trousers ? They all immediately go into a scrum to make sure that no one can see, while they produce another pair of pants. That's how bankers behave when they see a default.
A British politician

It's so expensive to be rich.

> *Susan Gutfreund, wife of John Gutfreund, then boss of Salomon Brothers*

I'm not a banker, I'm a thespian.

> *Dennis Levine, banker, who was jailed for fraud*

These were the 1980s, remember, the decade of excess, greed and materialism. I became a go-go guy, consumed by the high pressure, ultra-competitive world of investment banking.

> *Dennis Levine*

The culture of the bank is criminal

> *Robin Leigh-Pemberton on BCCI*

If you don't have some bad loans you are not in business.

> *Paul Volcker, former boss of the Federal Reserve*

Wholesome is the best word to describe Nick. I married him for better, for worse, for richer, for poorer.

> *Lisa Leeson*

No apologies to anybody, for anything. Apologies don't mean shit. What happened, happened.

> *John Gutfreund, who resigned from Salomon Brothers following a scandal in the bond market*

For all its rogue charm (it) is a fairly nauseating piece of myth-making... It fails to wash – but celebrity crime being what it is, he will probably take over from Ronnie Biggs as guest vocalist when the Sex Pistols re-reform next century.

> *David Kynaston reviewing Nick Leeson's account of the Barings fiasco*

When you are the liquidator of a bank, you are liquidating a live animal rather than a dead one.

Christopher Morris, insolvency specialist

A vision of interdependence and interrelationship, a bridge where all people of the world come together on a single platform joining hands in mutual respect, togetherness and work for mutual benefit – creating a bold future embodied in one world, one nation and one bank.

Part of the mission statement of BCCI

You can't do good business with bad people and you can't get hurt with good people. That's all there is to know.

Howard Sheperd, banker at Citicorp

The stuff that novels are made of. This is not some boutique firm going under.

Gerry Grimstone, banker, on the collapse of Barings

3

DEBT

One of the things investors have learned about emerging markets recently is that they are hard to emerge from in an emergency.

> *Robert Hormats, of Goldman Sachs, reflecting on the economic crisis in Mexico in 1995*

A billion dollars isn't what it used to be.

> *Nelson Bunker Hunt, whose family incurred debts of $1,825 million after failing to corner the silver market in the 1980s*

Minus Millionaire.

> *Jim Slater's description of himself after the collapse of Slater Walker.*

I didn't lose any friends after after the crash, because I didn't have any that were just friends because of my position. I wasn't on the cocktail party circuit, so there was no denouncement.

> *Jim Slater*

There was no doubt that I had begun to believe some my own publicity. I was constantly reading in the newspapers how clever I was and on many occasions being referred to in the City pages as "the master". It was very heady stuff and without doubt it affected me.

> *Jim Slater*

Capitalism without bankruptcy is like Christianity without Hell.

Frank Borman, former chief executive of Eastern Air Lines

Companies do not go bankrupt the way they used to to, and countries are not declared in default. We talk about restructuring instead. We are prolonging the pains. We are postponing deaths. We are preventing new dynamic structures being created when others die. I think this is detrimental. We cannot abolish death.

Pehr Gyllenhammar of Volvo

People have the spending power but they have no money.

Allan Jones, Chicago taxi driver

Bankruptcy is a legal proceeding in which you put your money in your pants' pocket and give your coat to your creditors.

Joey Adams, comedian and writer

We pay the debts of the last generation by issuing bonds payable by the next generation.

Lawrence J Peter, educationalist

Yesterday is a cancelled check, tomorrow is a promissory note, today is ready cash.

Hubert Tinley

You know how it is in this country: when someone loses he immediately says he was cheated.

Richard Gordon on the Philippines

Countries do not go bankrupt.

Walter Wriston, banker

The bombing has stopped but they haven't got round to bayonetting the wounded.

An insolvency practitioner's response when asked if he feared redundancy now the recession was over.

Marvellous woman by the way – not to bail me out. Like me she believes in free enterprise.

Sir Freddie Laker on Margaret Thatcher after the collapse of his company

Insolvency practitioners make their living out of other people's misery and I've always regarded myself as a parasite. But we can't all be surgeons.

Michael Jordan, insolvency expert

There is absolutely no suggestion that we will not have enough money to mend the library roof. This is not going to mean soup at high table. We are not upset. Trinity is a fairly wealthy institution.

Dr. John Bradfield, senior bursar of Trinity College, Cambridge, following the collapse of Polly Peck, in which Trinity held more than 300,000 shares.

Nobody can learn how to be a businessman only by reading Mickey Mouse and Donald Duck.

> *A friend of tennis hero Bjorn Borg whose business empire collapsed*

I don't know where the money went – it just went. I don't even like shopping.

> *The Duchess of York*

I am going to sign on. I am penniless.

> *Ernest Saunders, former boss of Guinness*

We have lost everything we have worked for over the last 40 years.

> *The wife of John Major's village shopkeeper, when made shopless and homeless*

I am totally gutted.

> *Trevor Osborne on the appointment of receivers to Speyhawk the property company he formed 20 years earlier*

If we committed a crime it was that we tried.

> *Sophie Mirman, founder of Sock Shop, after the collapse of the company*

A remarkably large part of any rescuer's time is taken up in coping with (some would say, fighting off) the very same banks whose money the rescuer is trying to recover.

> *Sir Lewis Robertson, company doctor*

They assume if they go broke they won't go broke. That's debilitative quality. You have to let them go broke.

> *John Reed, banker, on Third World debt*

Ford to New York: Drop Dead.

> *New York Daily News headline after President Gerald Ford refused to bail out the city as it neared bankruptcy in the 1970s.*

CREDITOR: One of a tribe of savages dwelling beyond the Financial Straits and dreaded for their desolating incursions.

> *Ambrose Bierce, The Devil's Dictionary*

DEBT: An ingenious substitute for the chain and whip of the slave-driver.

> *The Devil's Dictionary*

It's not very glamorous, I suppose. But it's rather like being a dustman – somebody's got to do it.

> *John Clementson, receiver*

It is just an ordinary bankruptcy with noughts on the end.

> *The receiver on the William Stern bankruptcy who had debts of £118,690,524*

What I liked about it was the element of personal confrontation. You would sit the man down on the other side of the table and try and get him to tell the truth. Often they wouldn't want to tell you. There are usually things they want to hide, like they are keeping a mistress or something. But it would be my job to find out; to break the man apart.

> *Bill Mackey, receiver*

A cynic has observed that if you go bust for £700 you are probably a fool, if you go bust for £7,000 you are probably in the dock and if you go bust for £7 million you are probably rescued by the Bank of England.

> *Lord Meston*

In Debtors' Yard the stones are hard
And the dripping wall is high...

> *Oscar Wilde, The Ballad of Reading Gaol*

It is unanimously and without qualification assumed that when anyone gets into debt, the fault is entirely and always that of the lender and not the borrower.

> *Bernard Levin, journalist*

I was honest. Being too honest in the business world is a defect.

> *Masao Ushida, president of Nihon Netsugaku Kogyo, after the company collapsed in 1974, then the biggest business failure in Japanese history.*

I shall miss my Rolls-Royce and yacht, but now I have peace of mind.

> *John Bloom, the washing machine tycoon of the 1950s and 1960s after his company crashed.*

I was, perhaps rightly, a dangerous upstart, an interloper in the well-regulated affairs in the City of London. Now was the chance to teach me a crushing and merited lesson.

> *Clarence Hatry, who was sentenced to 14 years in prison for fraud in the 1920s*

You could say that I feel resigned now that all the harassment is over. We had as much advanced warning as the United States government at Pearl Harbour.

> *William Zeckendorf Sr, US property developer, after the banks pulled the plug.*

When you English see a loophole in the law you drive a mini through it. I, Savundra, drive a Rolls-Royce.

> *Emil Savundra, who was jailed for fraud after his Fire Auto and Marine insurance company went bust in 1966.*

All we can do for the third world is to give them Mr. Yamani's telephone number.

> *Felix Rohatyn, US banker*

If there's one thing worse than being exploited by multinational corporations, it's not being exploited.

> *Saying in the third world*

Debt isn't good, debt isn't bad. To put it in the extreme, for some companies no debt is too much leverage. For others a debt of 100% can easily be absorbed. People assume the capital structure of a company is burned in stone. The capital structure, like the individual, is constantly changing.

> *Michael Milken*

How can they say I'm bankrupt? I owe a million dollars.

> *William Zeckendorf Sr.*

If he keeps going like that he'll be broke in 250 years.

> *H.L.Hunt after hearing that his son was losing $1 million a year owning a football team*

Saving New York city from bankruptcy is like making love to a gorilla. You don't stop when you're tired; you stop when he's tired.

Felix Rohatyn, banker

Credit buying is much like being drunk. The buzz happens immediately and gives you a lift. The hangover comes the day after.

Dr. Joyce Brothers, psychologist

No country has ever been ruined on account of its debts.

Adolf Hitler

A nation is not in danger of financial disaster merely because it owes itself money.

Andrew Mellon, US financier and politician

Blessed are the young, for they shall inherit the national debt.

Herbert Hoover

You've got to like people. When I call it may be at a distressing time – often more so for me than for them – and if you're insensitive, you're in the wrong job.

Nicholas Guest, bailiff

Peace has not been good for our business.

American arms dealer Robert Bright explaining why he went bankrupt

I stand here today a bankrupt with a great deal of humility. Bankruptcy is a very public humbling.

Kevin Maxwell

There was no Toscanini. There is no Beethoven. It was more like Arnold Schönberg improvising as he composed.

> *Donald Regan, then US Treasury Secretary, on the handling of the Mexican debt crisis in 1982*

I've never been able to understand how the Democrats can run those $1,000-a-plate dinners at such a profit and run the government at such a loss.

> *Ronald Reagan*

There's been no change in my lifestyle.

> *Japanese tycoon Dr. Kichinosuke Sasaki on his debts of £2.3 billion*

It has long been my deliberate judgement that all bankrupts of whichever denomination, civil or religious, ought to be hanged.

> *Charles Lamb, essayist*

There's no wolf at the door yet. All it means is that we are working eight-hour days instead of twelve-hour days. There are still big names out there that are in trouble.

> *Steve Hill, receiver, on the downturn in his industry following the improved economic situation*

I will remember your government. I will do all in my power to ensure that your bungling and arrogance is always brought to the public's notice... what a ghastly group of incompetents you are.

> *Elizabeth Smart, businesswoman and lifelong Tory supporter, in a letter to John Major following the collapse of her company*

History is bunk, the future is junk.

> *Saying*

4

MISBEHAVING

The moral fibre of the Japanese people has deteriorated, and they have become desensitised towards money.

> *Seiroku Kajiyama, Japanese government minister, on the collapse in the copper price following the discovery of the Sumitomo Bank*

I have done a terrible thing. I have made a terrible mistake. I have been insider dealing.

> *Geoffrey Collier, stockbroker at Morgan Grenfell, admitting he had been a naughty boy, was fined £25,000 and given a suspended prison sentence.*

I just want to say I am deeply ashamed and I do not understand my behaviour. I have spent the last year trying to understand how I veered off course.

> *Ivan Boesky, who was jailed for three years and fined $100 million dollars for insider trading*

"I realise that by my acts I have hurt those who are closest to me…" He could go no further. Tears welled up, his face flushed and his voice broke. To the astonishment of a packed court, Milken started crying like a baby, his slight body wracked by involuntary sobs. "I am truly sorry," he blurted out but the rest of his statement was lost amid anguished cries and the sight of his lawyer, Arthur Liman, helping him to sit down.

> *Michael Milken, the inventor of junk bonds, breaking down in court after pleading guilty to six counts of securities fraud.*

You take home pastrami every night for free. It's the same as information of Wall Street.

> *Dennis Levine, disgraced insider trader, comparing his activities to those of a grocery worker*

Today in February 1990, the Drexel empire looks like the Thousand Year Reich in May 1945. Like an imprudent householder, Drexel has entered the protection of Chapter 11 of the Federal Bankruptcy Code. It has defaulted on at least $100 million of short-term debt. Thousands of staffers are seeking new jobs. The company has no credit on Wall Street. That most anomalous of situations has happened: a securities company whose capital was largely in its own issues has had to admit the worthlessness of its own issues.

> *Benjamin Stein, journalist*

The era of extravagance and insanity has come to an end. This is a breath of fresh air. Drexel got what it deserved. These guys could destroy the country. There was no rhyme or reason for what was going on.

> *Pierre Rinfret, economist*

Don't steal; thou'll never thus compete successfully in business. Cheat.

> *Ambrose Bierce*

Money is lacking? Well then, create it!

> *Goethe*

When I heard the phone ring it sounded like the ding of a cash register.

> *Dennis Levine*

He was an indefatigable and pesky spider whose web grew ever stickier and once I had crossed the line, I was hopelessly entangled.

> *Dennis Levine on Ivan Boesky*

I can't predict my demise, but I suspect it will occur abruptly.

> *Ivan Boesky*

They say the best definition of a mine is a hole in the ground with a liar standing on top of it.

> *Julian Baring*

My husband is a rat. He's settled, he's fine. I'm the one holding the bag, the innocent party who's never done anything.

> *Seema Boesky, wife of disgraced Ivan during divorce proceedings*

Overnight I went from being someone who was socially acceptable to a social outcast. I saw my name removed from buildings. Charities returned my cheques. Clubs requested our resignations.

> *Seema Boesky*

What's the difference between Robert Maxwell and the average pension fund trustee? Maxwell knew what he was doing.

> *A joke doing the rounds   after the discovery of Maxwell's pension fraud*

It is sad that a lot of problems the country is in today are mixed up with my problems

> *Michael Milken*

British justice has been done.

> *Roger Levitt, boss of Levitt Group, who was sentenced to 180 hours community service after admitting fraudulent trading prior to the collapse of his company with £34 million debts.*

If the judge and the prosecution thought I should have gone to prison, I guess that is what would have happened. They were marvellous. They are nice people.

> *Roger Levitt*

All these years, I thought the marketplace or the customer was the final judge. I was wrong. In the short run, it's the media. And in the media, nothing means anything unless it's negative.

> *Michael Milken*

Nor should we forget Robert Maxwell, the Monster, if only to remember that you could add up all the sins of all MPs, multiply them a hundredfold and only then equal Maxwell's crimes.

> *David Mellor, former MP*

You need to rent an MP just like you rent a London taxi.

> *Lobbyist Ian Greer to Mohamed Al-Fayed*

Anyone who can be bought is not worth buying. I know that now.

> *Mohamed Al-Fayed*

My conscience is very, very clear.

> *Robert De Lorean*

My original idea was to do ostrich farming but the bottom has fallen out of that now.

> *A former businessman who started a naturist bed-and-breakfast in Wales*

They bonk three times a day, seven days a week for seven months of the year.

> *Brian Ketchell, managing director of the collapsed Ostrich Farming Corporation*

It seems that City history has been made. Where shall I be able to read all about it ? In the Guinness Book of Criminal Records.

> *Lady Sachs at the end of the Guinness illegal share support operation trial*

You can tell that our economy is improving at last. For the first time someone has been arrested for counterfeiting the Hungarian currency.

> *Geza Jeszensky, Hungarian foreign minister*

Lord Iveagh said he was in favour of anything which would restore the Guinness family to where it should have been. He said that if the Guinness family had done in its second hundred years what it had done in the first hundred, remembering that it was not only a brewing concern, but into finance as well, then the business would have been up with the Rothschilds.

> *Ernest Saunders, the former chief executive of Guinness, giving evidence during his trial for operating an illegal share support operation during the takeover bid for Distillers*

The likes of Robert Maxwell don't succeed without the cooperation of cowards.

> *Anne Robinson, journalist*

Every time some businessman is caught engaging in fraud, for some reason the public likes to blame the minister who probably doesn't know anything about it.

> *Nicholas Ridley, then Trade Secretary*

A thing worth having is worth cheating for.
W C Fields

The louder he talked of his honour, the faster we counted our spoons.
Ralph Waldo Emerson

He was like a nuclear physicist isolated in Los Alomos in 1944, so focused on splitting one atom, so assured that his work would help win the war that he couldn't see that he might be creating a lethal instrument capable of jeopardising his own security.
Marie Brenner, on Michael Milken

A sickness I have in the face of which I am helpless.
Ivan Boesky

In white collar situations, they don't think of themselves as thoroughgoing criminals, so when they get caught there's a level of guilt involved. Suddenly there is a conflict between what they appear to families, friends, co-workers, and what they are doing in the secret part of their life. It tends to move them towards confessing, putting it all behind them. They haven't acquired the ethics of organised crime which is that you never help the government, constantly trying to frustrate it.
Rudolph Giuliani, US prosecutor

Inside traders are just another set of hoodlums. With one difference – they roll much easier
Rudolph Giuliani

Only Al Capone, according to the Guinness Book of Records, could sustain a claim to have exceeded Mr. Milken's income – and he was self-employed.

The Wall Street Journal after it was revealed that Michael Milken had earned $550 million in one year

Fraud is infinite in variety: sometimes it is audacious and unblushing; sometimes it pays a sort of homage to virtue; and then it is modest and retiring; it would be modesty itself if it could only afford it. But fraud is fraud all the same.

Lord MacNaghten

Your parole office has not been born yet.

Edwin Torres, a New York judge, to a convicted fraudster

I say to wives who have husbands aiming at the stars. "How badly do you want that Jag or Porsche, that holiday home and so on?" You may get them, but you may not have a family any more. I have been there and I wish I hadn't.

Ernest Saunders, disgraced former boss of Guinness

You have a very high standard of fraud in your country. Basically, you have to steal the Crown Jewels and get caught before you call it by that name. But if the people at Lloyd's behaved like this in the USA they would be in the penitentiary with Boesky and Milken.

Dr. George Pakozdi, a Canadian dentist and Lloyd's Name

The junk bond market, as least as we have come to know it, is dead. For the past half dozen years, it has been a creature less of rational financial precepts than of wishful thinking, artful promotion and above all illusion and magic… Instead of free interaction of buyers and sellers, the market was ruled tightly by sorcerers – Michael Milken and his apprentices at Drexel Burnham Lambert Inc.

Business Week

I know that in the wake of today's events many will call for reform. If my mistakes launch a process of reexamination of the rules and practices of our marketplace, then perhaps some good will result..

Ivan Boesky

I was subjected to the most inordinate number of MPs looking for free flights, upgrades: 'Can I bring the wife?' they'd say, 'I'll be going over to Bangkok for the weekend.'

Disgraced lobbyist Ian Greer

I have built my enterprises on the firmest ground that can be found – the foolishness of people.

Ivar Kreuger, the match king

Whenever I'm caught between two evils I take the one I've never tried before.

Mae West

The thing I would most like to see invented is a way of teaching children and grown-ups the difference between right and wrong.

Robert Maxwell in 1985

Fuck 'em.

Lord King as he retired as chairman of British Airways following the Virgin Atlantic's allegations of dirty tricks

If Richard Branson had worn a pair of steel-rimmed glasses, a doubled-breasted suit and shaved off his beard, I would have taken him seriously. As it was I couldn't.

Lord King

If the government showed a little bit more of the enthusiasm they have for pursuing minor social security frauds in looking at the major problems that arise in the City, it would do us all a lot of good.

John Smith, then shadow Chancellor, on the Polly Peck affair

I am not bitter. I am more perplexed than anything else.

Neil Hamilton, whose political career was ruined following allegation of sleaze

I am perplexed that Mr. Hamilton is perplexed... It is a very perplexing perplexity.

Martin Bell, who won Hamilton's seat in the 1997 general election

Robert Maxwell

5

BAD GUESSES

Stock prices have reached what looks like a permanently high plateau.

Prof. Irving Fisher, economist, a few weeks before the 1929 crash

Invest in silver and you can never go wrong.

Nelson Bunker Hunt, who lost billions after his attempt to corner the silver market went wrong

Britain is coming out of recession. The green shoots of economic spring are appearing once again.

Norman Lamont at the 1991 Tory conference

I've never bothered trying to cultivate an image in the City, although I guess someday I might have to start. Maybe I've even gone too far in the past to upset people because I just can't stand the boors you find there. They drive me around the bend with their stuffy non-committal approach.

Gerald Ratner, then boss of Ratner Group

My biggest mistake was to turn down the opportunity in 1989 to bid for the rights to the Teenage Mutant Ninja Turtles.

Bryan Ellis, managing director of Hasbro UK

I will stick to the facts and statistics. The poetry can come later.

Norman Lamont when asked about the green shoots of economic recovery

We are more likely to see little green men than little green shoots.

Tony Banks, MP

(Norman) Lamont lied about the green shoots of recovery. There are more green shoots in a pot noodle.

Richard Littlejohn, journalist

I remember when Bill Gates visited me to sell me MS DOS, his operating system. I told him we couldn't take such a retrograde step.

Hermann Hauser, the founder of Acorn Computers

Ratner's has got very little to do with quality. We do cut-glass sherry decanters with six glasses on a silver-plated tray – and it only costs £4.95. People say how can you sell this for such a low price. I say because it's total crap. There is no point beating about the bush. We even sell a pair of gold earrings for under £1 which is cheaper than a prawn sandwich from Marks & Spencer. But I have to say the sandwich will probably last longer than the earrings.

This comment by Gerald Ratner cost him his job and nearly broke the company.

In future there will be no more jokes. I'm going to join the clan of boring businessmen. It's a shame, I know, having to sound responsible and careful.

Gerald Ratner.

All my financial worries are over.

Sir Freddie Laker a few days before the banks pulled the plug

I have my name on the side of the plane. It has got to do well.

Sir Freddie Laker

On to Little Bighorn for glory. We've caught them napping.

General Custer

The fact that I was never wrong created character flaws that caused me to make mistakes.

Paul Reichmann, property developer

On a scale of one to ten if the risk with the World Financial Centre was nine, here it would be one.

Paul Reichmann, on the Canary Wharf development which ultimately brought him down

The only question that enters our minds is: Will success happen immediately or later ?

Paul Reichmann, at the ground-breaking of the Canary Wharf project

My religion won't allow me to go to Las Vegas. This is my Las Vegas.

Paul Reichmann, who is Jewish

The poorhouse is vanishing among us. We in America today are nearer to the final triumph over poverty than ever before in the history of the land.

Herbert Hoover a year before the great depression

You are as safe with me as you would be in the Bank of England.

Robert Maxwell

6

PROBLEMS

It would have been cheaper to lower the Atlantic.
> *Lord Grade on the failure of his film Raise the Titanic*

I remember once being asked to try to think about my failures
but I could not think of any failures
> *Bruce Gyngell, television executive*

Failure is both a funny and a sad thing. We worry so much about
it coming our way that we cultivate ulcers, nervous
breakdowns, tics, rashes or hot flushes. Yet, on the odd occasion
when that dark day of doom does come around, we find it isn't
really quite as bad as we thought it would be; for some reason,
the way our minds sometimes tend to work overtime building
up possible disasters is very often far off the mark.
> *G Kingsley Ward, Canadian businessman*

If all else fails, immortality can always be assured by spectacular
error.
> *Prof. John Kenneth Galbraith*

You can't run a Church on Hail Marys.
> *Archbishop Marcinkus, former head of the Vatican Bank*

A recession is when your neighbour loses his job. A depression
is when you lose yours.
> *Ronald Reagan*

I don't know anything about any depression.

> *J.Pierpont Morgan in 1930*

The farmers will come up smelling of roses as usual, but we will be forgotten. We are at the base end of the industry. We just work quietly and get on with it.

> *Graham Reed, chairman of the little-known Association of Cattle Head De-Boners, whose industry was wiped out by the BSE crisis.*

Just as no one would buy a used car from Richard Nixon, no one would eat a hamburger laid on his plate by a British cabinet minister.

> *German newspaper Tageszeitung during the BSE crisis.*

You think you're superman, you think you can do anything. I felt invincible and that there were no limits as to how late I could stay up or how much I could travel...

> *Larry Kudlow, chief economist at Bear Stearns, who confessed to battling with drug and alcohol addiction*

King was effectively calling me a liar so I sued him.

> *Richard Branson on Lord King*

It is important to preserve this essential ingredient of our epicurean heritage.

> *Ipe Jacob, receiver at Clarke Foods*

It was crazy in the 1980s. There were a bunch of businesses which were narrowly focused, undercapitalised and run by inexperienced people. There was even one chain called Tooth Booth, selling brushes and dental floss. What do you think happened to that ?

> *Roy Bishko, boss of Tie Rack*

Richard Branson

If you are going to dump, don't dump a financial journalist if you are the deputy governor of the Bank of England. That's dumb.

> *Journalist Mary Ellen Synon, whose affair with Rupert Pennant-Rea led to his resignation*

The Bonk of England.

> *Sun headline describing the affair*

They have acted like a bunch of shits.

> *John Major on his European colleagues during the BSE crisis*

The bottom's gone out of the market.

> *Arnold Taylor, seaside postcard artist on falling sales*

We were the willing, led by the unknowing, doing the impossible for the ungrateful.

A worker at the doomed Swan Hunter shipyard

Most football teams take their own chef with them and take their own food with them for a variety of reasons, because the eating habit of a football team is often reflected in the way it plays on the pitch, which is probably why our football plays crap.

Labour MP Tony Banks reacting to the news that the German football team was insisting that its beef be imported from Germany during Euro '96 because of the BSE crisis

We will bounce back. We are the barrow boys of the City.

Gary Stevenson, a former employee of Morgan Grenfell

Tradition dictates that we have a lawn – but do we really need one? Why not increase the size of your borders or replace lawned areas with paving stones ?

Advice from Severn Trent Water during the water shortage crisis in 1996

I realise it isn't a lot, but every little helps.

An elderly traveller who sent £20 to Eurotunnel following the fire which caused £50 million worth of damage

Sell off the British Isles to Brother Frog, say, for nuclear testing, and we would be economically out of the woods in no time.

Satirist John Wells

I am not a great fan of capitalism. But I am a realist.

Fidel Castro on his economic reforms

The period of market romanticism has ended for us. We must make our people's lives easier.

> *Viktor Chernomyrdin, Russian prime minister*

I can't think of anybody who might want to buy the company – except Father Christmas.

> *Retail analyst Mark Husson on the troubled Sock Shop*

Once we had socialism without social justice. Now we have capitalism without capital.

> *Polish satirist Jan Pietrzak*

Virgin Screws BA

> *Sun headline*

The group had reported a pre-tax profit of £90.4 million for 1991, but after a change in accounting policies today revised that to a loss of £56.3 million.

> *Report on Queens Moat Houses*

This was mental aggression that boxing doesn't even come near to inflicting. It was a mental mugging.

> *Former boxer George Walker on the meeting at which he was ousted as boss of Brent Walker*

We have a very small sticks and no carrots.

> *Boris Fyodorov, Russian finance minister*

Our guards are as upset as anyone.

> *A Group 4 spokesman after the company lost three chickens which were eaten by a fox*

There's always a fear in working class people that all the success and adulation has just been a dream and that you'll wake up tomorrow morning back where you started.

Adam Faith

The death of endeavour and the birth of disgust.

Ambrose Bierce on achievement

A man is not finished when he is defeated. He is finished when he quits.

Richard Nixon

Forecasting is very difficult, especially when it's about the future.

Saying

Our analysis leads us to believe that recovery is sound only if it does come of itself. For any artificial stimulus leaves part of the work of depressions undone and adds, to an undigested remnant of maladjustment, new maladjustments of its own.

Joseph A Schumpeter, economist

I know all about problems. I grew up in the 1930s with an unemployed father. He didn't riot. He got on his bike and looked for work. And he found it.

Lord Tebbit

There was time when a fool and his money were soon parted but now it's happening to everybody.

Adlai Stevenson

I cannot give you the formula for success but I can give you the formula for failure: try to please everybody.

Herbert Bayard Swope, journalist

Nice guys finish last.
> Leo Durocher, sports coach

Show me a good loser and I'll show you a loser.
> Paul Newman, actor

The trouble with the rat race is that even if you win you 're still a rat.
> Lily Tomlin, writer

He who hesitates is last.
> Mae West

Paul Newman

This tastes like a fart.
> Ross Johnson, then boss of RJR Nabisco, on the tobaccoless cigarette created by his company

I'm used to this kind of environment. We do a lot of business in Sicily.

> *Mari Cristinia Busi, boss of Coca Cola in Albania, on doing business in her war-torn country*

When we got into office the thing that surprised me most was to find that things were just as bad as we'd been saying they were.

> *John F Kennedy*

I've come down flat on my arse, but I'm going up again and this time I'm staying up.

> *Robert Maxwell after an early setback*

A man can be destroyed but not defeated.

> *Ernest Hemingway*

I think it's important to have a good failure when you are young.

> *Walt Disney*

Well, sometimes you just don't like somebody.

> *Henry Ford II explaining why he sacked Lee Iacocca*

Next to a battle lost, the greatest misery is a battle won.

> *Duke of Wellington*

I am humble enough to recognise that I have made mistakes but politically astute enough to know that I have forgotten what they are.

> *Michael Heseltine*

Too old to rock ' n ' roll and too young to fly.

> *Lord King on Richard Branson*

If you're not part of the steamroller you're part of the road.

Rich Frank of the Walt Disney Co

Our greatest glory is not in never failing but in rising up every time we fail.

Ralph Waldo Emerson

The minute you start talking about what you're going to do if you lose, you have lost.

George Shultz, statesman and industrialist

Most of us would rather risk catastrophe than read the directions.

Mignon McLaughlin, writer

Waiting for supply-side economics to work is like leaving the landing lights on for Amelia Earhart.

Walter Heller, economist

A lot of Americans think if it's made in Japan, it's terrific, if it's made in America, it's lousy. It's time to peel off the Teflon kimono.

Lee Iacocca, former boss of Chrysler

A nickel ain't worth a dime any more.

Yogi Berra, sports coach

Licensed to swill

Newspaper headline after lottery company Camelot revealed that directors were to receive huge bonuses

There seem to be few signs that any of their leadership contenders have learnt the hard lesson that the downsizing of the Conservative Party followed their enthusiastic support for downsizing everyone else.

John Monks, TUC general secretary

I feel like Custer being shot at from all sides. Maybe it's because I'm flamboyant, maybe it's because I'm a Democrat, maybe it's because I was a bachelor for a long time, maybe it's because I'm Jewish.... I have no idea.

Marvin Warner, whose Ohio Home State Savings failed

Let's be optimistic, fellows. After all, the only thing we have to fear is fur itself.

Myron Cohen, a comedian from the garment industry, on a depression in the fur trade

There is nothing like losing all you have in the world for teaching you what not to do. And when you know what not to do in order not to lose money, you begin to learn what to do in order to win

Edwin Lefèvre, business writer

The worst moment in my career in the funeral business had to be in 1988 when I was being presented to the Queen with Alan Sugar, Gerald Ratner and Richard Branson. Just as I was leaving the hotel the phone went and I heard: "We've buried the wrong body in Worcester."

Howard Hodgson, former undertaker

Watch sex. It is the key to success and the trap door to failure.

Michael Shea, former press secretary to the Queen

The instability of the economy is equalled by the instability of economists.

John Henry Williams, writer.

In the end, the blame was all mine.

Paul Reichmann after the failure of his company Olympia & Yorke

Some people were just stupid. People were booking weddings around their two free tickets. How dumb can you be?

Sacked Hoover chief Brian Webb on the disappointed customers in the company's free flights fiasco

We tell our managers, "Don't be afraid to make a mistake. But make sure you don't make the same mistake twice."

Akio Morita, then CEO of Sony

7

INFLATION

The road to inflation is paved with good intentions.

William Guttmann, writer

Writing all these noughts made work much slower and I lost any feeling of relationship to the money I was handling so much of. It had no reality at all, it was just paper. We had to sort so many different kinds of notes and count them. And if it didn't come out right we had to stay on at night and count and count again. It might be a million that was missing, but after all it was worth nothing.

Lisa Frank, a bank clerk in Germany during the great inflation of the 1920s

The old marks were burnt in the courtyard of the bank. The books were changed – it was all very easy. But I found it afterwards very boring. When it was normal I didn't like it. I just didn't like it. I was young then, 22 years old. The work was boring, everything was boring. It had been so exciting just to throw money away on things. One can learn that money really just isn't anything.

Lisa Frank

One town issued money consisting of leather suitable for soling shoes as a truly inflation-proof kind of currency.

William Guttmann on the fashion for creating their own banknotes in certain regions of Germany during the great inflation of the 1920s

The towns and villages also indulged in a little political propaganda on their notes, particularly during the struggle against the occupation of the Ruhr, by printing anti-French slogans and caricatures on them.

William Guttmann

Through credit to riches.

Phrase during the great inflation of the 1920s in Germany

Two examples indicate how inflation hit people in Berlin: on 16 July 1923 the price of a tram ticket was 3,000 marks; on the 30th, 6,000; on 6 August, 10,000; On the 14th, 50,000 and on the 20th, 100,000.

Gill Anton

Some turned for survival to crime. The most easily saleable commodity, which required no capital investment, was sex. In many once respectable apartments, sex clubs sprang up; the manager was the paterfamilias, the madam the mother and the whores their daughters.

Gill Anton

Banknotes became literally not worth the paper they were printed on. Because they were printed on only one side, minor entrepreneurs set up ad hoc stalls bartering them as scrap paper.

Gill Anton

Inflation is a disease, a dangerous and sometimes fatal disease, a disease that if not checked in time can destroy a society.

Prof. Milton Friedman

Inflation is a great moral evil. Nations which lose confidence in their currency lose confidence in themselves.

Lord Howe

Inflation means that your money won't buy as much today as it did when you didn't have any.

Anon

Inflation is repudiation.

Calvin Coolidge in 1922

Bolshevism was caused largely by the changes in the buying power of money.

Lord d'Abernon

Inflation is like sin. Every government denounces it and every government practices it.

Sir Frederick Leith Ross

Inflation might be called prosperity with high blood pressure.

Arnold H Glasgow

People who do not regard inflation as the greatest evil are an exotic species here; they do not last long.

Thomas Buch, head of personnel at the Bundesbank

Central bankers are against inflation like priests are against sin. But few are out and out fundamentalists.

Guy Quaden, banker

Inflation is when there is too much month left at the end of your money

John Major MP

Inflation might be called legal counterfeiting.

Prof. Irving Fisher, economist

In a sense there had been an inversion of values. Money and success were now seen as goals that justified breaking the law, while honesty was stigmatised because it flew in the face of the rules of dog-eat-dog inflationary society. The shifts in the relative standing of the different social groups that we have described not only made individuals uncertain about their social status but also helped foster a widespread new relativism in social morality.

Detlev J K Peukert, writer, on the great inflation in Germany in the 1920s

Among the members of the independent professional classes – doctors, authors, journalists, actors – having two jobs is now virtually the rule; people are running round in all directions for ways of earning money: the leisure which used to nourish intellectual activity and permit the cultivation of ideas is no more; the sense of security in old age, that cushion for those who live on their wits and nerves, has vanished; and the landscape is dotted with poor, hunted creatures, roaming in fear of the spectre of poverty, no longer able to offer disinterested service to the life of the mind.

S. Saenger on the German inflation in the 1920s

Inflation makes balloons larger and candy bars smaller.

David Kurtz, American writer

The government fighting inflation is like the Mafia fighting crime.

Lawrence J Peter, educationalist

We have a love hate relationship. We hate inflation, but we love everything that causes it.

William Simon, banker

Inflation is the parent of unemployment and the unseen robber of those who have saved.

Margaret Thatcher.

Inflation is as violent as a mugger, as frightening as an armed robber and as deadly as a hit man.

Ronald Reagan

Inflation is a form of taxation that can be imposed with legislation.

Prof. Milton Friedman

Inflation is worse than communism

Lord Kingsdown, formerly Robin Leigh-Pemberton

Inflation isn't an Act of God. High inflation is a man-made disaster, like Southern beer and nylon shirts.

Ronald Long, consultant and professional Northerner

I do not think it is an exaggeration to say history is largely a history of inflation, usually inflations engineered by governments for the gain of governments.

Prof. Friedrich Hayek

Not every German believes in God, but they all believe in the Bundesbank.

Jacques Delors, then president of the European Commission

Lenin was right. There is no subtler, no surer means of overturning the existing basis of society than to debauch the currency. The process engages all the hidden forces of economic laws on the side of destruction and does it in a manner which not one man in a million is able to diagnose

John Maynard Keynes

There were lots of concerts because people from abroad with hard currency... would come to Berlin and engage the Philharmonic Orchestra for what to them was virtually nothing. You could buy yourself a concert for $100.

Gill Anton

Alan Clark

8

LLOYD'S

I joined because it was a very English thing to do. I didn't even need the money. I never made an assessment of what I was doing – which I know doesn't let me off the stupidity of it. I didn't even understand what a broker was. I did understand what unlimited liability was, but I was told it was just a joke,

Fernanda Herford, a Lloyd's name.

But in any case the people who have made losses are not the kind who are used to making a fuss. Quietly, there's a lot of suffering, but it's a very English sort of suffering.

Tom Benyon, former MP, on Lloyd's of London

When they come down to Tennessee to collect the money, I'll have both guns loaded. You know, as far as America is concerned, Lloyd's can just go whistle Dixie.

Henri Weddel, Memphis stockbroker and Lloyd's name

Insurance? These are the spivs who ripped the widows to pieces in Lloyd's, put your premium up by twice the rate of inflation every year and last week actually had the arrogance to stage a conference on how to contest policy-holder's claims.

Alan Clark, MP

Of course I can't pay it. I have already sold my nice Kensington home. I am now living in digs in Barnet. I used to have two aeroplanes. Now I have a bicycle.

Clive Francis, a Lloyd's Name

I can't escape the feeling that if the gentlemen of Lloyd's (of London) were Eastenders dealing in used cars they'd be behind bars by now.

Diane Abbott MP

I had deposited a large sum of money so that Baring's could issue a bank guarantee to Lloyd's [of London] so I could continue trading as a "Name".
But now I'm told it has been frozen. I simply can't believe my bad luck. I have lost money for three years running – and now this happens...I just think that people ought to know that when they go into a bank to deposit some money...some young trader in Singapore can gamble it away on something called derivatives.

Michael Stearn

There is no cavalry coming over the hill bearing dollops of money.

David Rowland, then chairman of Lloyd's of London

It's the greatest name in the insurance world and we have sullied it.

David Rowland

What Lloyd's (of London) has lost forever, is a certain sort of Englishness on which it once prided itself and which was coincidentally good for business. In the first place, it will have lost its money base in Arabella's pony land, that world of second homes, private incomes and private education. Beyond this, Lloyd's will have lost – has already lost – its peculiar, arcane, mystical, sexy status among the segment of British society it once did so well by; for want of a better word, it has lost its honour – beyond or at least beside, such motives as snobbery, greed and supposed canniness –

that brought in the rush of new Names in the Eighties; and in the dishonouring of Lloyd's they have lost their shirts.

Julian Barnes, writer

When I was growing up, the thickest men I knew went into Lloyd's. At school, I had a friend who couldn't even get into the Navy. He took his maths O-level five times and failed five times. He joined Lloyd's. I should have thought then and there.

An anonymous Lloyd's Name

Only my arrest prevented me from completing the formalities (and perhaps saved me from bankruptcy).

Roger Cooper, who was jailed for five and a half years in Iraq

My father was killed in the war and my grandfather in the war before that. I look and see what I've done to the land and I think how can I go and meet them.

A ruined Lloyd's Name

The numbers now are just academic really. We can't pay. The thing is that if you are drowning in the Atlantic or a pond – you're still drowning.

Norbert Mallet, a ruined Lloyd's Name

When I joined (Lloyd's), the byword was fidentia. Someone put an "L" in the middle and now it's fiddlentia.

Clive Francis

I was told that all the ships in the world would have to sink on the same day to lose even our deposits, and that the talk of cuff links was an anachronism, a joke and it really meant nothing.

Canadian dentist Dr. George Pakozdi, a Lloyd's Name

I can't afford a suit. I have lost weight. My health is deteriorating and my family faces bankruptcy. I stand before you as a victim, a loser.

Chartered accountant Anthony Groman, a Lloyd's loser

The 300-year-old principle of *uberrima fides* – utmost good faith – started to be replaced by the principle of *caveat emptor*, as if you were buying a used car from Arthur Daley.

Alfred Doll -Steinberg, a Lloyd's underwriter

I never joined Lloyd's because all the stupidest boys I was at school with seemed to go into it and that worried me.

Max Hastings, journalist

Lloyd's is the only casino where after you have walked out they follow you and take your house away.

Michael Deeny, chairman of the Gooda Walker Names Action Group

The pity for the Names is that few outside Lloyd's sympathise with them. The rich have no public constituency.

An observer on the Lloyd's debacle

Q: How do you make a small fortune at Lloyd's ?
A: Start off with a big one.

Lloyd's joke

Lloyd's always argued that the unlimited commitment of its members was one of its strengths. I have long thought it a weakness and a delusion – one of those quaint old British customs so widely envied that nobody copies it.

Christopher Fildes, journalist

There used to be something about Lloyd's which appealed to a certain type of American Anglophile. So when Lloyd's went about aggressively expanding its base of Names in the 1980s and wooing the newly-monied, many normally hard-headed American businessmen were smitten. They were flown to London and put up in underwriter's flats, wined and dined, and their wives taken to matinee shows in the West End. They glimpsed a world of style and sophistication which looked irresistible from the perspective of small town America. The whole concept of Lloyd's was so marvelously quaint. Even the traditionally Lime Street caveat, that unlimited liability means you are liable "down to your last cuff link" appeared heroically dotty and British.

> *Stephen Robinson, journalist*

You wake up at five in the morning and think it can't work out like that. You've got this ghastly despair. It takes over sometimes when you're out gardening or when you go to dinner. You suddenly think: "that bloody Lloyd's".

> *Richard Godden, a ruined Lloyd's Name*

Insurance should be a very dull business. We never had any publicity for years. It was a very dull place.

> *David Coleridge, then chairman of Lloyd's of London*

Lloyd's has got a Clint Eastwood syndrome — lots of men with no Names.

> *Tom Tickell, business writer*

I'm an accountant. I read all the accounts before joining, that's what I'm most angry about.

> *Michael Deeny, Lloyd's Name and chairman of the Gooda Walker Names Action Group*

I don't like being swindled. I'm from Northern Ireland. I don't mind a fight.

> Michael Deeny

My wife has divorced me, I have had to take my children out of public school and I have had to sell my Ferrari.

> Alan Price, a ruined Lloyd's Name

The sums now needed are usually only obtained with a mask, a gun and a getaway car.

> A spokesman for the Society of Names on the financial demands being made of Lloyd's Names

When are you going to accept Lloyd's is full of overpaid, incompetent and greedy men who make double glazing and timeshare salesmen look like amateurs ?

> Sally Noel, a Lloyd's Name, to David Rowland, its chief executive

Lloyd's recent history is an outrageous disgrace with greed, bad management, incompetence and catastrophes bringing the market to its knees. Lloyd's has been bewitched, battered and bewildered to such an extent that its capacity to survive is in real doubt.

> James Sinclair, managing director of Willis Faber & Dumas

Life has become a burden because you're never at peace, you're never at rest, you can't relax, you get ill. I'm practically physically sick when the postman calls because I don't know what he's going to bring.

> Denys Axelberg, Lloyd's Name

Don't worry your pretty little head.

> Assurance given by Brian Bell, Lloyd's agent, to 21-year-old widow Bridget Milling Smith before she joined Lloyds.

A mob of upper-class bookies with a mild talent for PR.
The New Statesman on Lloyd's.

It's human nature to get greedier and greedier and greedier.
Ian Posgate, former Lloyd's underwriter

Ask not for whom the Lutine bell tolls. It tolls for Lloyd's.
The Economist

We are being asked to pay losses on policies written before we were born, to set up reserves to pay claims which will arise after we are dead, surely there is no doubt as to where the reasonable answer to the question: "Should I pay or not ?"
Tom Benyon, Lloyd's Name

What we are dealing with here is a unique combination of greed, criminality, and incompetence.
The Daily Telegraph on Lloyd's

Remember this face – I hope you have nightmares over it it.
A ruined Name to the chairman of Lloyd's

As Eli Wallach said to Steve McQueen: "If God had not meant them to be sheared he would not have made them sheep."
Robert Hiscox, a managing agent at Lloyd's on Names

You don't have to commit incest because your mother is the only other person in the house.
Sir Peter Green on possible conflicts of interest in Lloyds.

If I could do a Lord Lucan, I would. It's a nightmare
Bill Brown, Lloyd's broker

We won't make you a fortune, but we won't lose you one either.
Tony Gooda's assurance to new Names

There are a lot of people who can't tell a loss from a scandal.
David Coleridge, then Lloyd's chairman

Lloyd's Fiddles While Names Burn
A legend on a banner outside an EGM at Lloyds

Dear Mr.Rowland, Thank you for your recent settlement offer, a document for which my wife and I have found a domestic use. We have only two objections to it, viz: the paper is too thick and shiny; there are no perforations where the pages join the spine. If you could rectify these omissions in future offers, you would not only save money on printing costs but also distribute further amenity to our hard-pressed household
A letter to the chairman of Lloyd's from a Name

Whenever life has looked a little glum in the last year or two, I have been able to console myself with the reflection that I am not a member of Lloyd's. Once upon a time smug, fat men sidled up to one on shoots and smirked horribly: "Just got the Lloyd's cheque. Very nice number – pays for the wife to go to Portugal with her boyfriend. You really ought to think about it."

"Now, of course, a frightful inverted snobbery has taken over, whereby everyone boasts about the size of their losses.
Max Hastings.

It's like the final scene in *Braveheart* : you get hung, drawn and quartered and you keep wondering when it's going to stop.
Max Prentice, a ruined Lloyd's Name

I can understand that sometimes people don't wish to come forward to us but if they would just pick up a telephone and see what we had to offer then they would realise there is no need to do anything so drastic as take their own life.

John Thompson, secretary of Lloyd's hardship committee

Robin Hood, because during the past two years I have been associated with making the rich poorer.

David Coleridge, then chairman of Lloyd's of London, replying when asked with which historical figure he most identified

There is no point feeling sorry for yourself, is there ?

Gilbert Russell, 74, who lost £200,000 as a Lloyd's Name and now earns £3.74 a week delivering newspapers

A piece of me is gone – but it's a tough old world and a lot of people are worse off.

Boxer Henry Cooper who had to sell his three Lonsdale Belts after his Lloyd's losses

I was recruited to Lloyd's at a riverside picnic in Africa. It was full of crocodiles, but they were not half as dangerous as the sharks at Lime Street.

Tony Ravenscroft, a Lloyd's Name

I can remember going to a cocktail party about four years ago. It was being held in a huge crowded room and a woman came up and asked me what I did for a living. When I said I was a Lloyd's underwriter she said at the top of her voice, 'Oh, you're one of those lying, cheating bastards.' The room went quiet. I thanked my host for a very nice party and left.

Stephen Catlin, Lloyd's underwriter

"Profits" The English have a way of saying the word 'profits' that is just divine. Even knowing all I had learned about Lloyd's, I felt I could listen forever to Lloyd's chairman David Rowland's voice as he said the word 'Profits'.

Elizabeth Luessenhop, a former American Name

Lloyd's at the moment needs leadership. It need someone to stop all this bickering and to deal with the tendency to hang on to the horse and cart when the car has been invented.

A Lloyd's member

There is blood up and down the shires. It's too horrible to contemplate.

A ruined Lloyd's Name

We do have in this country one priceless advantage over actual and potential European competitors. And that priceless advantage which we should never spurn or lose is the international fame and standing of Lloyd's of London.

John Major in 1991

I find the Lloyd's saga extraordinary. Sensible people who would never go near a betting shop, a dog track or the Monte Carlo casino were seized by a collective madness. In the mid-1980s, more than 30,000 members of the British middle classes hurled themselves into a rerun of the South Sea Bubble and the Great Crash. They fell under the spell of Mammon and invited the ruin of their generation. Now they are selling their estates, their houses, their pictures, their boats. It is a redistribution of bourgeois property to lift the heart of a socialist.

Simon Jenkins, journalist

In spite of all our experiences of broken promises we are going to trust you again. Fleeced sheep have only their shepherd to turn to.

> *Christopher Stockwell, chairman of the Lloyd's Names Association Working Party, following the agreement to allow corporate investors into Lloyds*

Give peace a chance.

> *Peter Middleton, then chief executive of Lloyd's, during an angry meeting with Names*

The train's crashing at the front, but at the back they're still drinking Champagne.

> *John Rew, analyst, on Lloyd's of London*

9

FOREIGN EXCHANGE MARKETS

We went into Latin America not knowing anything about the place. Now we are leaving without knowing anything about it.

> *A Wall Street money manager on the crisis in the peso in 1995*

It has been a one-way street for sterling since 1931, a catalogue of disaster whichever government was in power. We are now weak even against the soft currencies in Europe. Once you are down against the drachma you really do have problems.

> *Neil MacKinnon, economist*

The Man Who Broke The Bank of England.

> *Newspaper headline on George Soros, who made a billion during the ERM crisis in 1992*

I could have made things more difficult but I didn't because I felt a certain responsibility not to destroy the European Monetary System.

> *George Soros*

Foreign exchange speculation is the Aids of the world economy.

> *President Jacques Chirac*

There are going to be no devaluations, no leaving the ERM. We are absolutely committed to the ERM.

> *Norman Lamont, then Chancellor of the Exchequer*

When Chancellors say they will never devalue, they are very often actually preparing for devaluation.

Sir Alan Walters, former economic advisor to Margaret Thatcher

Today has been an extremely difficult and turbulent day. Massive financial flows have continued to disrupt the functioning of the ERM... the government has concluded that Britain's best interests are served by suspending our membership of the ERM.

Norman Lamont

I've never taken drugs but I'm pretty sure this is what it feels like. You're on a high. It's tremendous. It's innovative, it's driving, it's second by second, it really is.

Doug. Bate, a foreign exchange dealer, during the ERM crisis in 1992

I don't give a shit about the Lira.

Richard Nixon during a run on the currency

This emergency measure, it must be recognised, clearly is in no sense a reflection upon the internal conditions of the country. It arises from the fact that foreigners, largely because of a lack of confidence in the stability of their own countries, have thrown such pressure upon sterling that it has become temporarily necessary to arrest the abnormal withdrawals of gold which have resulted.

The Bank of England explaining Britain's departure from the gold standard in 1931

Richard Nixon

I thought it was a hell of a day when the first rate rise came. But when the second hit us, the place went mental.

Foreign exchange dealer Darren Swords reflecting on the day Britain left the ERM

This is where the lions of the currency market work, where they circle the ailing wildebeest that is sterling. In a vast room they sit at tiered banks of pine desks. Atop the jumble of computer screens on every desk is a little flag denoting the currency in which the occupants deal. It looks exactly like the European parliament chamber, except there is real power here.

Jim White, journalist, describing the scene at National Westminster Bank's currency dealing room during the ERM crisis in 1992

You suddenly have all this sterling which is dropping in value by the second and you have got to get rid of it. In this game you stand to risk as much as you gain. People who criticise us for casting patriotism aside should come into the real world.

> *Paul Curle, foreign exchange dealer, rejecting criticism that he and fellow dealers undermined Britain by selling sterling during the ERM crisis in 1992.*

So the speculators rule OK? And to think we used to worry about government by the unions.

> *N. Ings. Letter to the Guardian after Britain's ERM withdrawal*

Many of us had begun thinking we would not have a job after 1996, when the single currency was due to come in. But now we have a job for a few more years.

> *Doug Bate, foreign exchange dealer, after Britain was forced out of the ERM*

On Wednesday I felt as though we were all part of history, and it was just great to be part of it. We have just had a week of historical importance, and it was wonderful to be involved in making it all happen.

> *Doug Bate*

The market thought the ERM was fundamentally weak. It wouldn't have mattered if you had Jesus Christ as Chancellor.

> *Doug Bate*

It's so volatile out there. The market is what we call whippy.

> *Mark Clarke, currency dealer, during the 1992 ERM crisis*

Up down, up down, who knows what's happening ? What is going on?

Gary Lyons, currency dealer, during the 1992 ERM crisis.

We did short a lot of sterling and we did make a lot of money, because our funds are so large. We must have been the biggest single factor in the market in the days before the ERM fell apart. Our total position by Black Wednesday had to be worth almost $10 billion. We planned to sell more than that. In fact, when Norman Lamont said just before the devaluation that he would borrow nearly $15 billion to defend sterling, we were amused because that was about how much we wanted to sell.

George Soros recalling Black Wednesday

From now on, the pound is worth 14% or so less in terms of other currencies. It does not mean, of course,that the pound here in Britain, in your pocket or purse or in your bank has been devalued.

Harold Wilson broadcasting to the nation following the devaluation of the £ in 1967

Grown men, professionals in a highly technical sense, masters of the slide – rule and computer in checking the odds of gain or loss on a foreign exchange transaction, allowed themselves a degree of credulity in simple matters of political fact which would have been scorned by a second former. Millions upon millions – millions of national assets – changed hands, drained for a short time out of the country, on an assumption – based on nothing more substantial than a gin and tonic or two – that I was at Buckingham Palace.

Harold Wilson following a run on the £ in 1968

Currency slaughter. The British pound, once worth 12 marks, slumped to 2.3 marks. You beautiful strong mark! You are making our lives cheaper. Handbags from Florence, insurance from London, leather jackets from Seville.

The German newspaper Bild celebrating the strength of the mark at the time of Britain's departure from the ERM

When a currency is felt to be weak, the markets will put the worst possible construction on any piece of news which might affect it – economic, political, or even industrial. I soon learned that there is not much point in complaining when the financial markets behave like hysterical schoolgirls. You cannot buck the markets.

Denis Healey, later Lord Healey, Chancellor of the Exchequer in the 1970s

I have had an excellent night's sleep and I feel fine. It has been the first time for some time that I had a night where I haven't had to worry about the pound.

Norman Lamont, after Britain left the ERM

There is going to be no devaluation, no realignment... I was under no illusions when I took Britain into the ERM. I said at the time that membership was no soft option. The soft option, the devaluer's option, the inflationary option, would be a betrayal of our future... It is a cold world outside the ERM.

John Major a week before Britain was forced out of the ERM

Mr. Lamont has acted with speed and courage in the unsuccessful struggle to keep the pound in the ERM.

John Major

Mr. Major must explain why the devaluation that less than a week ago was being condemned as a betrayal is today portrayed as our salvation.

Gordon Brown, then shadow Chancellor

It's like there is a death wish; people want a devaluation and no one in the foreign exchange markets is going to be happy until there is a devaluation.

Neil Blackley, analyst

The sky is darkening with the wings of chickens coming home to roost.

Lord Callaghan, after Britain left the ERM

They should accept the decision of the market they worship.

Denis Healey, later Lord Healey, former Labour chancellor of the exchequer. on the ERM debacle

Gordon Brown

We smelled blood when the doubts began about the Treaty of Maastricht, but we actually tasted blood with the lira last weekend. Now there is no stopping us; every time Britain, Italy or Sweden raise interest rates, it is like sprinkling a bit more blood into the pool.

Foreign exchange dealer

Italy offered us a map leading to a treasure. All we've had to do was follow it again in Britain and the treasure at the end was guaranteed.

Foreign exchange dealer

The last two or three days have been a total and utter defeat for the Euro chattering classes across all parties. If there is any suggestion of returning to the ERM it will be like a dog turning to its vomit.

Dennis Skinner

I've nothing against [George] Soros personally; I don't know him, he appears on TV and makes a nice impression. But if Mr Soros and his hedge fund can effectively force us to leave the European exchange rate mechanism, there must be something wrong.

Henry Grunfeld, president of SG Warburg

It is just as if Norman Lamont had personally thrown entire hospitals and schools into the sea all afternoon.

Central Banking magazine on the ERM crisis in September 1992

Realignment is another word for devaluation. We are not going to devalue the pound.

Norman Lamont, 5 January 1992

Leave the ERM, cut interest rates and let the pound find its own level… it's the cut and run option. The credibility of our anti-inflationary policy strategy would be in tatters.

Norman Lamont, 10 July 1992

Devaluation would lead to a collapse in market confidence and a damaging rise in interest rates. Withdrawal from the ERM would see a huge fall in the pound and an explosion of inflation.

Norman Lamont, 3 September 1992

Britain will take whatever measures are necessary to maintain sterling's parity.

Norman Lamont, 16 September 1992

The fact that we are outside the ERM at the moment does not mean that we are changing our policy at all.

John Major or Norman Lamont, 26 September 1992

When money is coming into a country it is called inward investment. When it leaves the country it is called speculation.

Julian Simmons of Citibank

The foreign exchange traders have done this country a favour. The UK's exchange rate was fundamentally overvalued and the government's policy unsustainable, so the foreign exchange market forced the government off that parity. It's a case of the ends justifying the means.

David Simmonds, economist at Midland Bank

When something like this happens people look for a scapegoat. Fifteen years ago it was the gnomes of Zurich: now it's the foreign exchange dealers. Uninformed public opinion has latched on to a simple response – blame the speculators.

David Simmonds on Black Wednesday

Devaluation, whether of sterling or the dollar, or both, would be a lunatic, self-destructive operation.

Harold Wilson

The Treasury's pro-ERM policy is like the robot in Terminator 2: you keep blowing it up, but it keeps coming after you.

A government advisor after Britain pulled out of the ERM

I felt safe betting with the Bundesbank. The Bundesbank clearly wanted the lira and the pound devalued, but it was prepared to defend the franc. In the end, the score was Bundesbank 3-nil; speculators, 2-1.

George Soros

The only thing that can save the franc now, without France hiking rates again or the Bundesbank cutting rates tomorrow, is Jeanne d'Arc.

Foreign exchange dealer David Wilson, in July 1993

The markets are operated by a mafia of gilded young lemmings who have square eyeballs because they never look at anything except a computer screen:they are interested only in numbers and they can never relate the numbers they look at to the economic realities which lie buried at the bottom of this heap of numbers.

Denis Healey, later Lord Healey

Mr.Major's quixotic battle with the speculators still seems the economic equivalent of the Charge of the Light Brigade: half a billion, half a billion, half a billion onwards

Times leader on the ERM fiasco

What do you have to do to be booted out of the cabinet? (David) Mellor gets away with rogering an actress. (Norman) Lamont gets away with rogering the economy. Do you have to roger every voter in the land before you get the boot?

Sun leader on the ERM fiasco

It seemed like the apotheosis of Tory economic policy: a Britain in which the only employment left was in foreign exchange dealing rooms; a service industry where we finally discovered a role – selling our own currency.

William Keegan, business writer, on the ERM fiasco

Market forces were in action. Adam Smith would have been delighted- all those unseen hands.

> *A dealer during the ERM fiasco*

There was no alternative. It had to be. I am a bit surprised that it took so long but I am not happy about the way it was done. If the UK was a public company the whole board of directors would have been fired along with the chief executive.

> *Sir Owen Green, then boss of BTR on Britain's departure from the ERM*

The government made no formal approach to the Bundesbank at any time for specific support for the Irish pound... you can't just ring up the Bundesbank and put the president under pressure. There is no clear process for lobbying the bank

> *Bertie Ahern, Irish finance minister*

As surprising as death at the end of a Greek tragedy.

> *The Independent on the devaluation of the Irish punt*

I am sure that I seem responsible for the sinking of the Titanic.

> *Norman Lamont in his last days as Chancellor of the Exchequer*

I am not an expert on the economy.

> *Norman Lamont*

I always get my threes and fives muddled up.

> *Norman Lamont*

My wife said she had never heard me singing in the bath until last week.

> *Norman Lamont a week after Black Wednesday*

I felt like one of those doctors in a soap opera on American television, where I was watching the monitoring of a patient's heart and I knew the patient was dead,

> *Norman Lamont, then Chancellor of the Exchequer, recalling Black Wednesday in 1992*

You might say that exchange rates are an indication of human wisdom And clearly show that human beings err often, and mistakes they make hurt people.

> *Toyoo Gyohten, chairman of the Bank of Tokyo*

A devaluation is never just an economic trauma. It is also a cultural milestone, a moment when a country catches a glimpse of itself in the mirror.

> *Michael Ignatieff, commentator*

Even on a quiet day it's organised chaos. It's like football, you can break your leg in a second and your career is over.

> *Gerrard Kelly, currency trader*

If governments do try to fix the currency it is the duty of the currency speculators to blow them apart. By doing that, they would do the world a very good turn.

> *Martin Taylor, Barclay's chief executive, seeking a postponement of the EMU start date*

If they revalue their gold, we'll revalue our monuments.

> *Clemente Mastella, Italian politician, protesting against Germany's plan to revalue its gold reserves in readiness for EMU entry.*

David Mellor

I blame David Mellor. He tipped off the market to try and get off the front pages.

A foreign exchange dealer during the ERM crisis in 1992

A man not in the Commons is a dead man.

Norman Lamont after he lost his seat in the 1997 general election

10

CRASHES

It's chaos. It's my funeral. I haven't been this scared for years.
Wall Street trader on the share price crash in 1989

It's total emotional and psychological chaos.
Eugene Peroni, Wall Street analyst on the same event.

It wasn't a crash, it was a meltdown.
John Phelan, the former chairman of the New York Stock Exchange on the 1987 share price crash

We're on a one-way escalator – down, down, down.
Australian stockbroker during the 1987 crash

Call it an inverse bull if you want.
London options trader on the 1987 crash

If I'd known that stock prices could fall so drastically I would have sold them earlier.
Japanese office worker after a sharp correction in Tokyo

It doesn't matter if share prices stop rising. I know how to play a downward market – in fact that's the best time to buy. The only thing that could go wrong would be if Wall Street collapses. That could bring me down.
Christopher Peach, then 16, who was ruined in the October 1987 share price collapse

I wish I hadn't required respectability. I'd be out selling the market short.

Joseph Kennedy

I wasn't affected by the crash of 1929. I went broke in 1928.

Gerald Lieberman, writer

New York is like a city with the plague. Every house is afflicted with the blight of withered stocks. The ruined market is the death-knell of a thousand hopes, and fear has replaced the light hearted gaiety with which New Yorkers a few months ago went about their business.

The Daily Mail reporting on the 1929 Wall Street crash

People gather at street corners, turning feverishly to the latest news of a fresh collapse, when only recently they could be seen pointing triumphantly to rising profits.

Ibid.

Rumours add their grim horror to the calamity, for scarcely an hour passes but there is a story that some well known broker or financier has committed suicide. The newspapers hide the news of self-inflicted deaths in different parts of the the papers, usually tagging to the tale some hint that the suicide was quite solvent at the time of his death. But the suggestion deceives nobody.

Ibid.

The brokers' offices are besieged with ruined speculators hoping to save some last mite from the crash. They are treated tenderly enough, for the brokers make no urgent repetitions for margin calls.

Ibid.

Freedom! The Reagan revolution is over. Death to yuppies.

> *A cyclist shouting at brokers in New York during the 1987 crash*

Maybe we should call it Fall Street.

> *A young broker in 1987*

My guts are numb. It's unreal, it's just unreal.

> *New York analyst Trude Latimer in 1987*

Like eight elephants trying to get through one door.

> *A New York dealer during a share price plunge in July 1990*

The market is in overdrive. It's a trillion-dollar yo-yo.

> *A New York analyst during 1987*

The Apaches were climbing the walls.

> *A Wall Street specialist recalling the 1987 crash*

After the Dow was down over 200 points on Black Monday people had that look you see when movies go into slow-motion. People were functioning, but they weren't relating to what was going on around them.

> *Art Cashin, broker, recalling the 1987 crash*

The atmosphere resembles restrained terror. The change in market psychology has been so sudden and so radical that no-one can really grasp it yet.

> *A New York broker after shares fell for the third session in a row in October 1979*

My wife and children ask me why I keep my gas mask and battle helmet and war souvenirs. Now they know. I'm wearing them.

> *Wall Street equity trader on the same event*

It's like slashing meat off my bones.

> *Factory worker Xu Kangyi, who lost the equivalent of four months' pay during wobbles on the Shanghai Stock Exchange in 1994*

A bear in a bull market is like a prohibitionist at a cocktail party. At first, some people take his admonitions to heart and sip soda water. But as the party goes on, nearly everyone joins in the drinking. Scorned, scoffed at, and – worst of all – ignored, the prohibitionist slips out to await the morning after.

> *Jeffrey Laderman, business writer*

A correction is when you lose money; a crash is when I lose money.

> *Larry Adler, businessman*

The non-event of the year.

> *Nigel Lawson, then Chancellor of the Exchequer, on the 1987 crash*

A crash is a primal shriek for the hard of hearing.

> *Bob Beckman, investment guru*

The situation has been reached in New York hotels where the clerk asks incoming guests "You wanna room for sleeping or jumping? And you have to stand in a line to get a window to jump out of."

> *Will Rogers, American humorist and actor during 1929*

On Fifth Avenue, police found a parrot screaming "more margin, more margin".

> *Wire service report during 1929*

Crashette.

> *A word used to describe something less than the real thing*

Mr. (Alan) Greenspan has just issued an euphoria warning.

> *George Magnus, chief international economist, on Greenspan's warning in December 1996 about the dangers of "irrational exuberance" on Wall Street.*

If we begin to create a stock market, this could unbalance our economic development. Therefore, we will not set up the market of capital in the near future.

> *Abel Aganbegyan, an economic advisor to Mikhail Gorbachev, during the 1987 worldwide share price crash*

You let me down.

> *Arthur Kane, an investor who lost a fortune in 1987, as he shot dead two Merrill Lynch brokers before turning the gun on himself*

This is one of the problems of wider share ownership.

> *A spokesman for the brokers that lent Christopher Peach, 15, £100,000 to invest in the Stock Market, which he lost and went bankrupt during the 1987 crash*

Nigel Lawson

Electronic automation and globalisation of the herd instinct.

> *Nigel Lawson, the Chancellor of the Exchequer, during the*
> *1987 share price crash*

Why should we Hong Kong patriots lose a lot of money at the expense of a bunch of New York Jews?

> *Ronald Li, then chairman of the Hong Kong Stock Exchange,*
> *defending his decision to close the stock exchange for four days*
> *during the worldwide share price crash in 1987*

There is no moral difference between gambling at cards or in lotteries or on the race track and gambling in the stock market. One method is just as pernicious to the body politik as the other kind, and in degree the evil worked is far greater.

> *Theodore Roosevelt*

In the autumn of 1929 the mightiest of Americans were, for a brief time, revealed as human beings. Like most humans, most of the time, they did some very foolish things. On the whole, the greater the earlier reputation for omniscience, the more serene the previous idiocy, the greater the foolishness now exposed. Things that in other times were concealed by a heavy facade of dignity now stood exposed, for the panic suddenly, almost obscenely, snatched the facade away. We are seldom vouchsafed a glance behind this barrier; in our society the counterpart of the Kremlin walls is the thickly stuffed shirt.

Prof. John Kenneth Galbraith

Trading is emotion. It is mass psychology, greed and fear.

Michael Marcus, trader

The market is nearly always wrong. I can assure you of that.

Michael Marcus

I was devastated. I felt like I was wounded in a trench and watching myself bleed to death. The market went limit-down five days in a row, and I lost over $600,000. On the fifth day, I remember sitting in a park holding hands with a girl I had picked up, literally crying on her lap. I was practically in a psychotic state.

Mark Weinstein, trader, after a bad day in the soya bean market

I was like a Sicilian whose wife had been murdered ten years earlier, waiting for the perfect moment for revenge.

Mark Weinstein

It was the day that the sun was so close to the earth that everybody needed zinc ointment and I was the only guy that had some left.

Tony Saliba, trader, who did well during the 1987 crash

General business throughout the country is fine and it should continue so indefinitely.

Thomas Cochrane, a partner at the J P Morgan in August 1928

Not many people were bullish at that point; I only know two others who were bullish. But you can't get that sort of buying opportunity very often. It's important to take advantage of it, if you have the guts and temperament.

David Lui, investor, on the Tiananmen Square massacre

No one likes a party spoiler, and as long as the stock market orgy goes on the pessimists are shunned as badly as AIDS carriers.

Marc Faber, investment guru

In the world of investment management, it is far better to fail very badly in a conventional way and lose a great deal of money for your client than to lose a little in an unconventional fashion

Marc Faber

The stock market, far more than a mechanism of investment or even legalised gambling, had carried for a great many middle-class people the prestige of capitalism itself. The market was the visible symbol of the rising line of "values" of property, even proof of some sort of classless society in the making, since investing had spread so widely through the country. When the market collapsed practically overnight, with none of the great leaders or institutions capable of stopping it or even understanding what was happening, a panic deep in the spirit made questionable any and all belief in anything official. In an act of contempt, someone thrust a midget onto the lap of the great and formerly sequestered investment banker J.Pierpont Morgan while cameras flashed. Other financiers landed in prison or jumped out of windows. The uncontrollable slide of the market also took with it what remained of the noble mythology justifying the First World War, which now became but another proof of the power of the moneybags to brutally squander innocent lives in order to make the rich richer. In this light the revolution in Russia, which had pulled the Czarist army out of the war and its mindless slaughter, made terrific sense; from a distance it seemed a sublime instance of man's intelligence.

Arthur Miller, playwright, on the 1929 crash

Too many people are apt to redeem their profits too quickly. In a huge bull market they wind up with piddling profits, only to watch their former holdings soar. That usually prompts them into making mistakes later when, believing that the market owes them some money, they buy at the wrong time at much higher levels.

Martin Zweig, investment adviser

What none of us can understand is why the world has gone into a tizzy.

Sir Nicholas Goodison, then chairman of the London Stock Exchange, during the 1987 crash

Nobody who has ever been on a falling elevator and survived ever approaches such a conveyance without a fundamentally reduced degree of confidence.

Robert Reno, analyst and writer, after the 1987 crash

It was paper when we started out and it's still paper afterwards.

Sam Walton on the 1987 crash

By tightening monetary reins now, they virtually ensure that the outburst the market so fears won't happen.

Jeffrey M. Laderman, journalist, just before the 1987 crash.

You can't be a bear on the United States.

A US industrial leader in mid-October 1929

In connection with various reports which have been industriously spread during the last few days, to the effect that a large bear pool has been formed, headed by myself and financed by various well known capitalists, I wish to state that there is no truth whatever in any such rumours as far as I am concerned, and I know of no such combination having been formed by others.

What little business I do in the Stock Market has always been as an individual and will continue to be done on such a basis. It is foolish to think that an individual or combination of individuals could artificially bring about a decline in the Stock Market in a country so large and so prosperous as the United States.

What has happened during the last few weeks is an inevitable result of a long period of manipulation of many stock issues to prices many times their actual worth, based on real earnings and yield returns. It is unfortunate for the general public when such a condition arises that real sound investment issues have to suffer to some extent along with issues of less merit.

If anyone will take the trouble to analyse the selling prices of different stocks, as for instance, United States Steel, which is selling around eight times its current earnings, many other issues must look, and have looked for a long time, as though they were selling for ridiculously high prices.

The Federal Reserve Board, through its various warnings, and many expressions from high banking authorities could not stop the market from going up. Hence it must be plain and seem utterly ridiculous for any sane person to presume that one lone individual could have any material effect on the course of prices of securities.

Jesse Livermore, US speculator during the 1929 crash

The present market decline is a healthy reaction which has probably overrun itself, and there is nothing alarming about it. In a market like this the fundamentals are the things to look for, and if you can show me anything wrong with the situation generally, then I would be concerned.

Charles E. Mitchell of the National City Bank a few days before the 1929 crash

Throgmorton Street last evening witnessed the the biggest and most exciting street market in Americans since pre-war days. The downpour of rain dissipated any inclination dealers in other markets may have had to linger after official hours, but this very factor served but to accentuate the congestion in the covered portion of Shorter's Court.

The market, which at other times would probably have overflowed into Throgmorton Street and the spacious well which forms the end of Shorter's Court, was compressed into such comparatively narrow dimensions as to constitute itself into a solid yet writhing mass of humanity. It was a rugger scrum on a massive scale, but without any space for the ball.

To penetrate to the heart of the market was a physical test, while those dealers whose business necessitated them remaining in more or less one position were continually subjected to the danger of fractured ribs. The conditions were such that, although Shorter's Court is merely a matter of ten feet or so across dealers on one side were at times totally unaware of the prices being made on the other. For instance, Hydros were 53 and three quarters on one side of the passage and 51 on the other. It was the tall man with the loud voice who put through his deals.

The cause of all this wild excitement was the cables received in the Stock Exchange towards the close of official business hours announcing that Wall Street had opened weak and was a seller of practically everything. In New York it was stated prices were being knocked down like nine pins.

Financial Times report on the 1929 crash

Believing that fundamental conditions in the country are sound and that there is nothing in the business situation to warrant the destruction of values that has taken place on the Exchanges during the past week, my son and I have for some days been purchasing sound Common stocks.

J D Rockefeller during the 1929 crash

You not only were arrogant, you were snobbish, and in lots of ways, very impolite and mean. …. Nobody likes you. You're Wall Street Yuppies and you've got a bad image…. I mean mostly north-eastern, Yale, Harvard types. You are mostly Republican. You were raised in Connecticut. You never ride the subways. So who gives a damn about you guys?

US talk show host Phil Donahue

I trusted him because of his family and because he had been to Eton.

Gwendoline Lamb, who lost £60,000 in Justin Frewen's company, Imperial Commodities

Wall Street is the gold rush of the 80s. Down there unless you are a millionaire by the age of 30, you're a failure.

Ira Sorkin, lawyer

Yuppies aghast at end of boom.

Times headline during the 1987 crash

October 19th 1987 was the day after Christmas and everyone wanted to return his stock certificates.

Arthur Kontos, president of Troster, Singer

A trader is always remembered for his losses, not his profits. It's always a joint decision with the man looking over your shoulder when you're right, and when you're wrong it's, "Why did you do that?"

John Arnold, trader

In a correction, other people's stocks go down; in a bear market, your stocks go down.

Alan Abelson, journalist

If you warn 100 men of possible forthcoming bad news, 80 will immediately dislike you. And if you are so unfortunate to be right, the other 20 will as well.

Anthony Gaubis

A broker is a man who runs your fortune into a shoe string.

Anon

When you lose on the stock market, don't blame the bulls or the bears but the bum steers.

Anon

There are old traders around and bold traders around, but there are no old, bold traders around.

Bob Dinda of Merrill Lynch

When a company president is ready to buy you lunch it's time to sell the stock. When he has something really good, you can't get him on the phone.

Phil Stoller

I don't know where speculation got a bad name, since I know of no forward leap which was not fathered by speculation.

John Steinbeck, writer

The average prudent investor is a greedy son of a bitch.

Anon

It's like being in the middle of a stock market crash.

A Tory supporter as the results flowed in during the 1997 general election

He's called a "broker" because after you deal with him you are.

Anon

The stock market, old boy? It's a hot bed of cold feet.

Anon

The government must express its love and concern for the stock market.

> *Hong In Kie, chairman of the Korea Stock Exchange, calling for tax breaks to revive Seoul's ailing exchange*

Wall Street professionals know that acting on "inside tips" will break a man more quickly than famine, pestilence, crop failure, political readjustments or what may be called normal accidents.

> *Edwin Lefèvre*

When things go wrong, they have a habit of going wrong everywhere

> *Leon Levy, investment banker*

A bear market is a financial cancer that spreads. Intermediate rallies (occasionally very strong ones) keep the hopes of investors alive. Furthermore, by continuously publishing bullish reports, brokers and economists, like good nurses, keep the flame of hope from burning out. But after 18 to 36 months of continued losses, total capitulation usually sets in and a major low occurs.

> *Marc Faber*

While the crash only took place six months ago, I am convinced we are past the worst.

> *Herbert Hoover*

I have no fears for the future of our country. It is bright with hope,

> *Herbert Hoover, in 1929*

This has been a twelvemonth of unprecedented advance, of wonderful prosperity... If there is any way of judging the future by the past, this new year may well be one of felicitation and hopefulness.

Herbert Hoover in 1929

(The Wall Street crash) doesn't mean that there will be any general or serious business depression. For six years American business has been diverting a substantial part of its attention, its energies and its resources to the speculative game....Now that irrelevant, alien and hazardous adventure is over. Business has come home again, back to its job, providentially unscathed, sound in wind and limb, financially stronger than ever before.

Business Week in November 1929

It was dreadful. I felt quite suicidal. The penny finally dropped with the brokers and they traced me to my school, threatening the headmaster with the Fraud Squad. My headmaster rang my mother and told her what had happened and I caught the bus home as usual and when I got off my mother was waiting for me, absolutely furious. My father was at the Motor Show in Birmingham and my mother had him paged to ring home immediately. He was more shocked than angry, he just didn't know which way to turn.

> *Christopher Peach, recalling how, as a schoolboy, he was wiped out in the 1987 share price crash*

It's a truth universally now accepted both in Monte Carlo and on Wall Street that when a gambler considers himself unbeatable he inevitably starts to lose.

Douglas Kennedy, business writer

How dreary the financial world would be without derivatives. There would be no romance, no poetry to make life tolerable for our investors.

Art Buchwald, columnist

Oh, the uses of adversity! In Washington the sound of the falling stock market was muffled by the scramble to reap political profit from financial failure. Almost everyone claimed that the market's rapid decline proved he had been right all along – about something or other and that the market was "calling" for just what he had already suggested.

Jeane Kirkpatrick, diplomat, after the 1987 Wall Street Crash

I was a boy during the crash of '29, but even then I don't remember such a panic as we've had this week. Then a penny would buy what a penny would buy and you could pretty much rely on it. But not any more.

Leather maker Henry Cooper on the ERM fiasco in 1992

WALL STREET: A symbol of sin for every devil to rebuke. That Wall Street is a den of thieves is a belief that serves every unsuccessful thief in place of a hope in Heaven

Ambrose Bierce, The Devil's Dictionary

Sometimes before I fall asleep at night I laugh out loud and kick my feet in the air at the absurdity of all this good fortune – from tyro philosopher to a real world wheeler-dealer overnight. When else in the history of mankind could a young man, just a few years out of school, become genuinely wealthy without taking personal risk or possessing unusual talents ? No doubt one day it will be outlawed. But for now I will enjoy the occasional, intense feeling that I've won some sort of sweepstake.

Jay Thomas, then 25

It's like a space shot or an assassination.
> *A New Yorker on the 1987 crash*

Sucker's rally.
> *Popular comment*

They have let the genie out of the bottle and on to the VDU.
> *Sir Kit McMahon, then chairman of the Midland Bank*

Up and down, up and down, what can you say ? It's minute to minute.
> *Joe Grundfest, a commissioner of the Securities and Exchange Commission, during the 1987 crash*

This is what happens when fear feeds upon fear.
> *A Wall Street analyst during the 1987 share price crash*

I don't know of anyone – are you talking about a specific case ?
> *President Reagan replying when asked what about the little old lady who lost money during the 1987 share price crash*

For some time the financial markets have acted as if the basic laws of economics have become inoperative.
> *Richard D Simmons, president of the Washington Post, during the 1987 crash*

We're doing a lot of handholding right now. I've never seen a day like this.
> *Steven Ross, broker, during the 1987 crash*

We're going through a very painful period, a wringout that's been due for two or three years.
> *Investor Doug Graham during the 1987 crash*

I watched Dad struggle through the Depression and the thing I learned was that you keep liquid and you don't owe money

> *Doug Graham, trader, who was a year old during the 1929 crash*

You saw some friends get wiped out. That's never pleasant. You saw a lot of blood.

> *Alan C. Greenberg, chief executive of Bear, Stearns during the 1987 crash*

What do you call a broker after a crash?
Hey, waiter.

> *Joke doing the rounds after the 1987 crash*

There are going to be a lot of yuppies delivering pizzas.

> *John Anderson, US politician, after the 1987 crash*

You know what they're calling yuppie stockbrokers today ? Puppies – poor urban professionals.

> *Jeff Bean, commodities trader, after the 1987 crash.*

What is frightening is that the computers have so much to do with it. One feels one's almost got into the hands of a robot.

> *Lady Acland, wife of the British ambassador to Washington after the 1987 crash*

I'm a little blown out. My intellect, which is now totally useless after today, tells me that the market may get a big lift tomorrow. But the markets can do what they want. They proved that today.

> *Mark Mehl, trader, during the 1987 crash*

Unless the world's coming to an end six months from now and we just don't know it, this market's out of whack. If the world's coming to an end I don't feel so bad.

Mark Mehl

Well, first of all, the indices, the index that is used for judging whether we're sound economically and so forth, has been up ten of the last eleven months. And with the great employment we have, with the fact that we have reduced that double-digit inflation and the prosperity that is ours out there, the one thing out of such a happening as the stock market that could possibly bring a recession would be if enough people, without understanding the situation, panicked and decided to put off buying things that normally they would be buying, postponing purchases and so forth. That could bring on a recession. This happened before.

But I don't think there's any real reason for that. I think that this was a long-overdue correction, and what factors led to its kind of getting into the panic stage, I don't know. But we'll be watching it very closely. I approve very much of what the exchange is going to do with regard to the next three days that the market is – trading is going on – and quitting two hours early to give them a chance to catch up with their paperwork, which is the reason for that. But this is, I think, purely a stock market thing, and there are no indicators out there of recession or hard times at all.

President Reagan commenting on the 1987 crash

What I felt mostly last week was oppressive fear. I felt as if I was present at the funeral. I realised, "My God, the kids, the car, the job, the career"

A Wall Street executive on the 1987 crash

I feel we've been to the brink and back.

A Wall Street executive

Once I built a railroad,
Now it's done –
Brother, can you spare a dime ?
Once I built a tower to the sun –
Brick and rivet and lime.
Once I built a tower,
Now it's done –
Brother, can you spare a dime?

Lines from a depression song, Brother Can you Spare a Dime?

This may be a short, sharp correction in the midst of an expansion or it may be the first signal of the next recession. We never claimed here that the business cycle had been abolished.

Robert Ortner, then US under secretary of commerce for economic affairs, during the 1987 crash

The public is suffering from brokers loanitis.

Mr. C E Mitchell during the 1929 crash

It was too amazing to be frightening.

Australian broker after the 1987 crash

There can be no doubt that the market has been too high in certain things. Now everybody will get to work instead of cherishing the idea that it is possible to get rich overnight by speculation, I think, however, that it has been a little drastic, but when the pendulum begins to swing it usually goes too far in either one direction or the other.

Alfred P Sloan, then boss of General Motors during the 1929 crash

I am still of the opinion that this reaction has badly overrun itself.

> C E Mitchell, chairman of the National City Bank during the
> 1929 crash

Weird Roar Surges From Exchange Floor During Trading In A Record Smashing Day.

> New York Times headline after Black Thursday in 1929

It was a mixture of groans, of hope and of sighs of relief. The final chorus had an eerie quality, like chords from a primitive requiem. And it meant the end of a day of pressure, of worry and of strain such as the exchange had never experienced.

> The New York Times' description of the end of business on Black
> Thursday in 1929 on the New York Stock Exchange

Now that the long pent up storm has broken we may reasonably expect sunnier days. The panic and crash were distinctly a result of specifically American conditions and American temperament. The moods of that people are apt to swing from one extreme to another.

> The London Evening Standard during the 1929 crash

We believe that present conditions are favourable for advantageous investment in standard American securities.

> An advertisement by brokers Hornblowers & Weeks the day after
> Black Thursday in 1929

It was not so much the little trader or speculator who was struck by yesterday's cyclone. It was the rich men of the country, the institutions which have purchased common stocks, the investment trusts and investors of all kinds. The little speculators were mostly blown out of their accounts by the long decline from early September. Thousands of them went headlong out of the market on Thursday. It was the big man, however, whose holdings were endangered yesterday and who threw his holdings into the Stock Exchange for just what they would bring, when hysteria finally seized him.

The New York Times during the 1929 crash

As bid after bid was filled for stocks and more and more offered, stocks of the best grade dropped almost perpendicularly.

The New York Times

It will send back to work many people who have been sitting around brokerage offices for a year or so on the trail of easy money. I have heard thousands of reports of merchants, farmers and men and women in all walks of life literally giving up their businesses to watch the stock market. Most of them will, by necessity, have to go back to earning their living in normal ways.

A banker during the 1929 crash

Almost anyone can lose his shirt on Wall Street if he's got enough capital to start with and the proper inside information.

Joseph Kennedy

The crowd always loses because the crowd is always wrong. It is wrong because it behaves normally.

Fred C.Kelly, stockmarket expert during the depression years

Any lack of confidence in the economic future of the basic strength of business in the United States is foolish.

Herbert Hoover in November 1929

The nation will make steady progress in 1930.

Herbert Hoover

The crisis will be over in 60 days.
>> *Herbert Hoover in March 1930*

The worst is over without a doubt.
>> *Herbert Hoover in June 1930*

We have hit the bottom and are on the upswing.
>> *Herbert Hoover in September 1930*

You can't expect to see calves running in the field the day after you put the bulls to the cows.
No, but I would expect to see some contented cows.
>> *A conversation between Calvin Coolidge and Herbert Hoover over the lack of results in the economy*

Failure is a matter of self-conceit. Men don't work hard because, in their self-conceit, they think they are so clever that they'll succeed without working hard. Most men believe that they'll wake up some day and find themselves rich and famous and eventually they do "wake up".
>> *Thomas Edison*

Money is made by sitting, not by trading.
>> *Stanley Kroll, commodities trader*

When good news about the market hits the front page of the *New York Times*, sell.
>> *Bernard Baruch*

Market orderly in record drop
>> *Wall Street Journal headline during the 1929 crash*

Stock market passes crisis.
> *Wall Street Journal during the 1929 Crash*

I am still of the opinion that this reaction has badly overrun itself.
> *C E Mitchell, banker, after Black Thursday*

The action of the market yesterday was reassuring and encouraging. The fact that a great volume of stocks was sold while prices remained comparatively steady was an indication of the sort of support the market will receive and the confidence of the important interests generally in business conditions and in the value of American securities.
> *Part of a letter sent to clients by brokers E F Hutton after Black Thursday in 1929*

Tokyo move fails to shake markets. Prices marked down but no heavy selling.
> *The Financial Times after the Japanese attack on Pearl Harbour*

Italy's declaration of war on the Allies had practically no effect in the City yesterday apart from the closing of Italian banks and marking down of Italian bonds.
> *The Financial Times*

I think these are lively testimonies to a continuing interest in St. Jude.
> *Dr. David Hugh Farmer, editor of the Oxford Dictionary of Saints, on the upsurge of notices in the Daily Telegraph thanking St. Jude. the patron saint of hopeless causes, in the wake of the 1987 crash.*

I can calculate the motions of the heavenly bodies, but not the madness of people.

Sir Isaac Newton, who sold out profitably during the South Sea Bubble but was tempted back in and lost £20,000.

When the crash came in the thirties, no banker would admit where he worked. Nobody wanted to work for a bank from 1933 to 1939.

Walter Wriston, banker

The world is made up of crazies and wise men. My crazy neighbour came up to me and said: "Why are you not putting your money in these schemes? Look what I am getting. So I became crazy."

An Albanian computer expert who lost all his money in a pyramid scheme

What is the market? It is the law of the jungle. And what is civilisation? It is the struggle against nature.

Edouard Balladur, former French prime minister.

There is no more mean, stupid, pitiful, selfish, ungrateful animal than the stock-speculating public. It is the greatest of cowards, for it is afraid of itself.

William Hazlitt

Anyone who tells you they always get the stock market right is either called George Soros or a liar.

Nick Knight, stock market strategist

They say there are two sides to everything. But there is only one side in the stock market; and it is not the bull side or the bear side, but the right side

Edwin Lefèvre

11

WISDOM AFTER THE EVENT

Share prices can go down as well as up.

Phrase used in ads. for financial services

October is one of the worst months to play the stock exchange. Other bad months are July, January, September, April, November, May, March, June, December, August and February.

Mark Twain

Wall Street is a street with a river at one end and a graveyard at the other.

Saying

Sell in May and go away.

Saying

It is agreed that to prevent the depression, the only method is to prevent the boom.

Lord Robbins

When speculation has done its worst, two and two still make four.

Samuel Johnson

There are two times in a man's life when he should not speculate: when he can't afford it and when he can.

Mark Twain

The elements of good trading are cutting losses, cutting losses and cutting losses.

Ed Seykota, trader

Short the industry which the majority of Harvard Business School want to join.

Marc Faber , investment guru

Let me again suggest that the future has never been clear to me (give us a call when the next few months are obvious to you – or, for that matter, the next few hours).

Warren Buffett in a letter to partners

With enough inside information and a million dollars you can go broke in a year.

Warren Buffett

Price is what you pay, value is what you get.

Warren Buffett

The first rule is not to lose. The second rule is not to forget the first rule.

Warren Buffett

Remember the only two investment principles that matter – what is isn't. What isn't is. Master this knowledge and no market can defeat you. Listen to the cry of the reptile deep within you.

The final sentence of financial strategist and writer Peter Tasker's novel

When you combine ignorance with leverage you get some pretty interesting results.

Warren Buffett on derivatives

Buy stocks like you buy your groceries, not like you buy your perfume.
> *Warren Buffett*

Don't go to a rich man for advice in a declining Stock Market
> *Saying*

Those of us who know nothing about the stock market will never understand it. That puts us right in the same class with economists and brokers who know all about the stock market.
> *James L Kilpatrick, journalist, after the 1987 crash*

Never give a sucker an even break
> *Saying*

A fool and his money are soon parted
> *Saying*

Man learns little from success, but much from failure
> *Arabic proverb*

The secret of life is honesty and fair dealing. If you can fake that, you've got it made.
> *Groucho Marx*

Men who don't take risks, won't drink Champagne.
> *Russian saying*

If you bet on a horse, that's gambling. If you bet you can make three spades, that's entertainment. If you bet cotton will go up three points, that's business. See the difference ?

Blackie Sherrode, sports writer

The best investment is land, because they ain't making any more of it.

Will Rogers

A study of economics usually reveals that the best time to buy anything is last year.

Marty Allen, marketing executive

Remember there are no bargains.

Anon

A bargain is something you have to find use for once you have bought it.

Benjamin Franklin

The buyer needs a hundred eyes, the seller not one.

George Herbert

Long term investments are usually short term investments which have gone wrong.

Anon

The only thing men learn from history is that men learn nothing from history.

Hegel

Wall Street is always the same: only the pockets change.

Jesse Livermore

Anybody who plays the stock market not as an insider is like a man buying cows in the moonlight
> *Daniel Drew, 19th century speculator*

The seeds of every company's demise are contained in its business plan.
> *Fred Adler, chief executive officer on Adler & Co*

The weather forecast has no effect on the weather. But the economics forecast may well effect the economy.
> *John Mason, businessman and diplomat*

Men don't plan to fail – they fail to plan.
> *William J Siegel, vice president of Printz-Biederman*

The cream rises until it sours
> *Lawrence J Peter, educationalist*

Never invest in any idea you can't illustrate with a crayon.
> *Peter Lynch, US investment wizard*

Don't make an enemy out of anyone you have sex with.
> *Psychologist*

The market, like the Lord, helps those who help themselves. But, unlike the Lord, the market does not forgive those who know not what they do.
> *Warren Buffett*

Always take a large pinch of salt when you talk to economists.
> *Economist Sir Alan Walters*

Debt is worse than poverty.
> *Saying*

When in doubt, don't
> *Saul W Gellerman, US academic*

It is better to pay a creditor than to give to a friend.
> *Aristotle*

Failure is the condiment that gives success its flavour.
> *Truman Capote, writer*

Failures are like skinned knees – painful but superficial.
> *Ross Perot*

Competence always contains the seeds of incompetence.
> *Lawrence J Peter, educationalist*

You can never go broke by taking a profit.
> *Meyer Rothschild*

Nothing recedes like success.
> *Walter Winchell, journalist*

There's a sucker born every minute.
> *P T Barnum*

Be awful nice to them going up because you're gonna meet them all coming down.
> *Jimmy Durante*

When ideas fail words come in very handy.
> *Warren Buffett.*

A small debt makes a man your debtor, a large one makes him
your enemy.

Seneca

Debt is the slavery of the free.

Publius Syrus

Creditors have better memories than debtors.

James Howell, writer

If fools went not to market, bad wares would not be sold.

Spanish saying

Never sell the bear's skin until you have killed the bear.

Saying

A lottery is a tax on imbeciles.

Italian saying

To open a business is easy; to keep it open is very difficult.

Chinese proverb

If at first you don't succeed try, try again. Then quit. There's no
use being a damn fool about it.

W C Fields

Never call a man a fool. Borrow from him.

Addison Mizner, architect

There's no such thing as a free lunch.

Prof. Milton Friedman

Don't get high on your own supply

Saying

Never pay the slightest attention to what a company president ever says about his stock.

Bernard Baruch, Wall Street legend

Don't sell stocks when the sap is running up the trees.

Addison Cammack, American trader at the turn of the century

Take care to sell your horse before he dies. The art of life is passing losses on.

Robert Frost, poet

Select stocks the way porcupines make love – very carefully.

Bob Dinda

Never invest your money in anything that eats or needs repairing.

Billy Rose

The ultimate risk is not taking a risk.

Sir James Goldsmith

Business patterns are perhaps the most volatile, the most voluntary and the most abstract of all groupings of mankind.

Miriam Beard, business historian

You can't buck the market.

Margaret Thatcher

An economy which habitually confuses financial engineering with the real thing is heading for deep trouble in the long term.

Sir John Banham, company director

What I accompanied was to change the flow of capital to those people who had the ability rather than those people who were born with money or who worked for large companies....I was focused on letting people feel they had a chance to participate. I think I was very successful in doing that.

Michael Milken

I could no longer endure constantly having to apologise for him; in fact, I felt as if I had to say ' sorry ' simply for being alive.

Elisabeth Maxwell on her husband Robert Maxwell

He was the Citizen Kane of his time. If you wrote a film about his life, it would be rejected as unrealistic.

Anthony Beaumont-Dark, former MP, on Robert Maxwell

He climbed 100 mountains and moved a thousand more.

Philip Maxwell on his father.

There were so many people who hated him. He had many threats. Many people would have been delighted to bump him off.

Elisabeth Maxwell on her husband Robert Maxwell

My life has been a failure.

Suicide note of Jesse Livermore, 1920s speculator. Livermore made and lost four fortunes during his life.

All the great economic ills the world has known this century can be directly traced back to the London School of Economics.

Dr. N.M. Perrera, former leader of the Sri Lanka Trotskyite Party and former student at the LS

INDEX

Page numbers followed by words in brackets indicate more than one reference on that page